Praise for Bases Loaded

"I just wanted to let you know I received the book and I think it is FANTASTIC!" — Jessica Mendoza, US Olympic Softball Team

"Thank you, Ms. Clanton, for helping me to spread the word about softball." — Jamie Gray, http://www.savesoftball.com

Other Title IX books by Barbara L. Clanton . . .

Live Love Lacrosse
Side Out

BASES LOADED

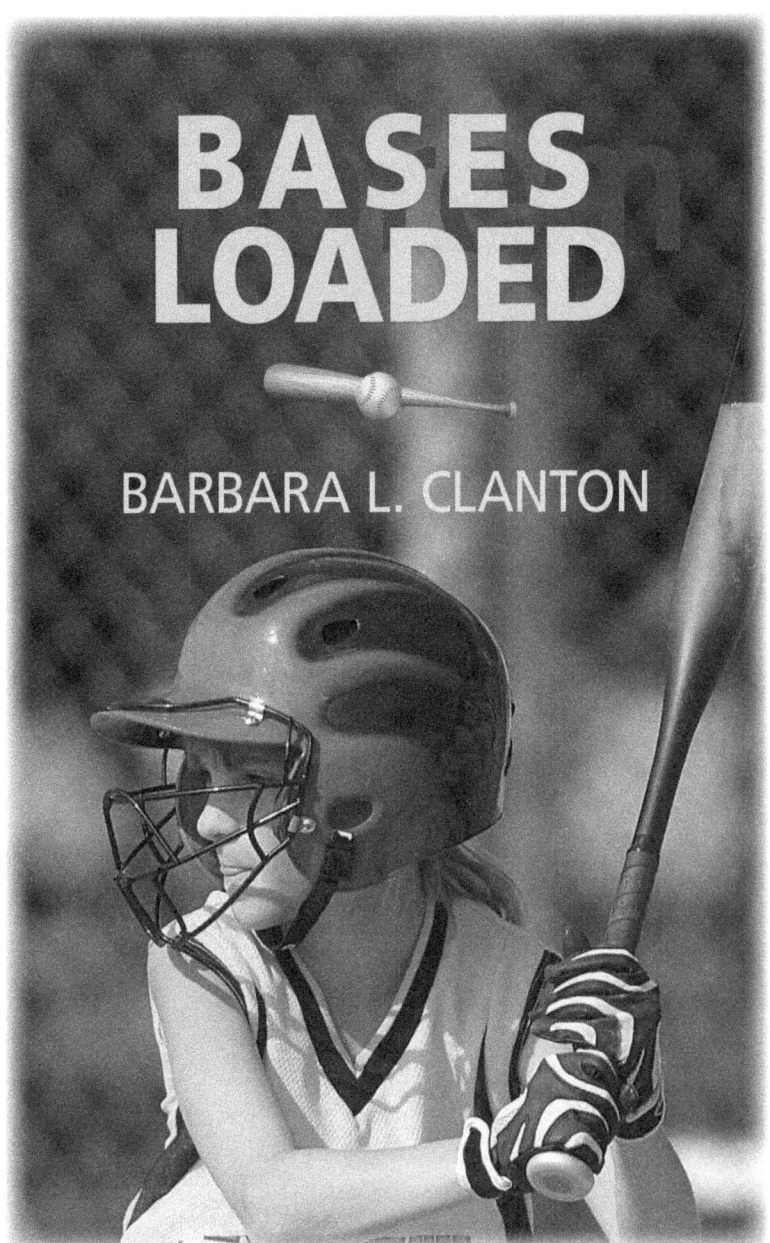

BASES LOADED

BARBARA L. CLANTON

A Dragonfeather Book
Bedazzled Ink Publishing Company * Fairfield, California

© 2009 Barbara L. Clanton

All rights reserved. No part of this publication may be reproduced or transmitted in any means, electronic or mechanical, without permission in writing from the publisher.

978-1-960373-35-9 paperback

Library of Congress Control Number: 2012914532

1st edition 2009
2nd edition 2012
3rd edition 2024

A Title IX Book

Cover Design
by
Sapling Studio

Dragonfeather Books
a division of
Bedazzled Ink Publishing Company
Fairfield, California
http://www.dragonfeatherbooks.com

Dedication

This work is dedicated to Jamie Gray and the Jamie Grays out there who have the guts to stand up for what they believe in. Jamie—with young people like you in the world, we're in good hands.

Acknowledgments

I had a blast writing this story and I have to first thank Carrie Tierney for suggesting the project to me. I appreciate the vote of confidence and the nudge for writing younger. I also want to thank my awesome Beta readers: dejay, Diana Schnitzer, Dorothy Boyer, Faith Hoffman, Tanner, Lucky Lady, and my folks Paul and JoAnne Clanton. You all had wonderful suggestions, comments and insights into the minds of twelve-year olds! Thank you. I also need to thank my colleagues Ralph Mazza, Dee Starling, and Georgia Parker for letting me pick their brains about youth softball. I am privileged to work with you all. Thanks also to the great folks at Dragonfeather. It was an honor to learn from you.

Chapter 1

Bag of Chips

Mackenzie Kelly adjusted her batting helmet and raised her bat. She waited anxiously for the signal from the coach. On the first day of tryouts, Coach Parks told them she rarely took sixth graders, but Mack was determined to make the team anyway.

Coach Parks held up her stop watch and yelled, "Go."

Mack swung the bat, aiming at nothing, dropped it to the ground, and sprinted toward first. The other girls cheered her on. She exploded toward second after using the new technique Coach taught them to round first base. She felt an extra burst of energy as she hit second and headed toward third. She was doing great. She just knew it. Her adrenaline kicked in as she approached third base, but just as she got ready to fly the final sixty feet to home plate, her foot slipped on the base and she was airborne. She braced herself for the landing.

"Oof," she cried when she hit the ground. She stared up at the January Florida sky, but regrouped in a hurry. She leaped to her feet and ran the rest of the way home.

She crossed the plate, and all the girls clapped and cheered for her, except one.

Sixth grader Halie Henri laughed out loud. "What a klutz," she said to her seventh grade friends. "She can't even run the bases."

Mack couldn't look at them, any of them. Tears stung her eyes. There was no way she'd ever make the middle school softball team now, and because of that she'd never make the Olympic team or win a gold medal either.

Coach Parks appeared out of nowhere and clapped her on the back. "You okay, kiddo?"

"Yeah, I think so." Mack didn't make eye contact with Coach Parks. She was too embarrassed.

"You were going pretty fast. In fact, even with falling, I think you beat out some of the other girls."

"Really?" Mack wasn't sure if Coach Parks was just saying that to cheer her up, but even so, it *did* kind of make her feel better. "Thanks, Coach."

"No problem, kiddo."

Coach Parks gathered the twenty-five or so sixth, seventh, and eighth graders around her. "I'll post the team roster outside the P.E. office tomorrow during lunch. You've made this an incredibly difficult decision for me, but don't be discouraged if you don't make the team this year, especially you sixth graders. I want you to try out again next year. Okay, that's it for today."

Mack's shoulders sagged. She didn't want to have to wait until next year. She had played soccer most of her life, but then her best friend Ashley Ames made her play softball the summer before. Ashley's dad had put together a team for the Winterford town league. Although Mack loved soccer, softball was way better. She could run, just like in soccer, but she could also hit and throw and catch and dive and slide. After playing softball in the twelve and under softball league, she was hooked.

Ashley grabbed Mack's arm and shook it vigorously. "Dude, do you think we'll make it? I'm so nervous."

"Pfft. Not with my fabulous fall back there."

"Oh, c'mon, dude. Coach Parks won't cut you just because of that."

Mack frowned. "You heard her. She wants sixth graders to try out again next year."

"She said to try out again if we don't make the team, and we're both going to make it. This year." Ashley took off her hair band and shook her dirty blonde ponytail free.

Mack sighed. "Halie will make it. They need another pitcher. She probably thinks she'll start, too."

"Yeah, no kidding. Halie thinks she's all that and a bag of chips."

Mack laughed and rolled her eyes.

"Oh, don't worry about her," Ashley said. "My dad says people who make fun of other people are just insecure."

"Whatever." Mack wasn't convinced. "Bag of Chips will make the team for sure, but there's no way Coach'll take you and me, too. She won't take three sixth graders." She sighed and threw her dad's old glove into her bag and then put the borrowed school helmet on the rack in the dugout. She pulled the rubber band out of her hair and raked her fingers through the dark waves.

"Hey, dude," Ashley said, "let's be positive about this, okay? What number do you want when Coach hands out uniforms?"

Mack couldn't stop her smile. "Ha! What do you think?"

"Oh, you're so predictable. Okay, number eight for you, but what if Halie wants Cat Osterman's number, too?"

"You and I both know that Halie will want twenty-seven for Jennie Finch. I mean, they're both blondes, and Halie wears that Jennie Finch hair band all the time."

"Yeah, but what if she—?"

"Okay, okay," Mack said. "If Halie takes eight, then I'll take two, Jessica Mendoza."

"That makes more sense, you know, because Mendoza's a left fielder like you. Or you could take twenty-nine—Natasha Watley. You run as fast as she does."

"I wish, but Watley doesn't fall down like I do. What number do you want, as if I didn't know?"

"Guess."

"Let's see, could it be three? The number of a certain second baseman on Team USA?"

"When Lovieanne Jung retires I'm taking her position and her number. But c'mon, my dad's probably holding his breath in the car, waiting to find out if we made the team. Too bad he has to wait another day."

"Yeah, too bad for us, too."

Mack picked up her bag, hoping she would need it for softball practice the next day. Otherwise, it was back to soccer full time.

Chapter 2

Dumb

Mack looked at the clock again. Ten minutes left of English. Ten long minutes until lunch. When the bell rang, she was going to run right past her own locker so she could meet Ashley at hers, and then together they would take the longest walk in the history of their lives down the corridor to the girls' P.E. office. Together they would find out if they had actually made the team, or if they would have to wait a whole year to try out again.

Mack blew out a big breath and tried for the thousandth time to focus on the story in her English textbook.

"Mackenzie Kelly?"

Mack jumped at the sound of old Mrs. Hendricks's voice. "Yes, ma'am?"

"Come up here, please."

Mack sighed as she put her book face down on her desk. She walked the death march to her English teacher's desk. She wondered how long Mrs. Hendricks had been torturing students this way. Probably since the beginning of time because her hair was gray, almost silver, and she always wore it up in an old-fashioned bun to match her old-fashioned clothes. Maybe her clothes were from colonial times when she taught George Washington. Mack tried not to laugh.

She could feel, rather than see, the other students watching her. Getting called to the front of the room was nothing new for her, and she could pretty much predict what Mrs. Hendricks was going to say. They had a test the next day after all.

"Mackenzie, last Friday's reading comprehension test was an abysmal failure as you know. I see now that I must somehow find a way to persuade you to take a more active role in your own education."

Mack felt her face flush. She wished Mrs. Hendricks would keep her voice down so the other kids in the class, especially Halie, wouldn't hear.

"Do you understand what I'm saying, young lady?" Mrs. Hendricks peered at Mack over the top of her old lady glasses.

"Yes, ma'am." Mack gave Mrs. Hendricks the answer she wanted even though she really had no idea how to take a more active role in her own education. She studied for every single one of those stupid reading comprehension tests. Every single one. But every time, she'd get no better than a C, usually worse. And lately, the tests were getting really, really hard, and she was having trouble getting C's.

"I hope you do understand, young lady, because at this moment you have a gentleman's D. Do you know what that means?"

Mack shook her head, but inside she thought it probably meant she was dumb.

"What it means," Mrs. Hendricks continued, "is that if you don't change your lazy ways, this generous grade will drop to the grade you truly deserve."

Mack sighed and looked at her feet. "Yes, ma'am, but . . ."

"Yes?"

She looked back up at Mrs. Hendricks. "I am trying. I just can't read as—"

"I don't want to hear any more of your excuses, young lady. Now go on back to your seat and put in a little more effort." Mrs. Hendricks waved Mack away from her desk.

"Yes, ma'am." Mack shuffled back to her desk and plopped down with a sigh. She had tried to tell Mrs. Hendricks that she just couldn't read as fast as everyone else and that when most of the other kids were on page five she was still on page two. She had always been the slowest reader in elementary school, but now that she was in middle school it was really beginning to show.

Halie whispered loud enough for Mack to hear. "Did you hear that? I knew it. She can't read."

Mack cringed when she heard the giggles behind her. She steeled her chin and thought, *I can read. I just can't read very fast.* She wished she had the courage to actually stand up to Halie Henri, but she didn't.

And Halie wasn't the only problem she had. How was she ever going to get into the University of Texas where Cat Osterman had gone if she had a "gentleman's D" in sixth grade English? When an answer didn't miraculously appear, she put her head down on the desk and counted the seconds before lunch.

Chapter 3

Center Field

The list hung on the bulletin board like some far away star that neither Mack nor Ashley could reach. Too many girls hovered around it, just as anxious to see if they made the team.

"How'd she get up there so fast?" Mack frowned.

"Who?"

"Halie."

"Bag of Chips?"

Mack laughed. "Yeah, Big Bag of Chips."

"I don't know." Ashley shrugged.

Halie made her way back out of the crowd, and the other girls congratulated her on making the team. *No surprise there*, Mack thought glumly.

Mack craned her neck. "Can you see?"

Ashley shook her head. "No, dude, too many people in the way. What's so hard about this?" She growled. "Read your name and get out of the way."

Halie bumped shoulders with Mack. "Actually, Ashley, some people around here can't read their own names, but since it's not on the list, what's there to read?" Halie fell back in step with her group of seventh grade friends, who had also made the team.

With an irritated hand, Mack brushed away the first sting of tears.

"Dude, don't worry about her. She's just a jerk. She's a big old bag o' chips."

"Yeah, I know. I don't know what her problem is." Mack waited with Ashley on the outer edges of the crowd. She wasn't so anxious to see the list now that Halie had said her name wasn't on it, but, still, she needed to see for herself.

"C'mon." Ashley pushed forward.

Mack stared at the list. She saw a lot of the eighth graders' names on it along with a few of the seventh graders'. Of course, Halie Henri's name was there. Mack smiled when she saw Ashley's name, but her heart broke when she didn't see her own.

"I made it. I made it." Ashley grabbed her arm. "Dude, I have to call my dad." She dug into her jeans' pocket and pulled out her cell phone.

"Congratulations." Mack heard the disappointment in her own voice. She wanted to be happy for Ashley, but that was hard when it felt like she'd just hit into a double play and lost the game for her team. Now she wouldn't ever play on the Olympic team with Cat Osterman or Jessica Mendoza or Natasha Watley. It was back to good old soccer again.

"What's wrong?" Ashley asked.

Mack pointed at the list. "I didn't make the team."

Ashley looked shocked. Mack followed Ashley's finger down the list. Ashley dropped her hand after the last name. She frowned. "I'm sorry. I thought for sure you'd make it even if I didn't. Dude, you're so much better than me. There's got to be a mistake."

"No, you heard what Coach said yesterday. Sixth graders shouldn't get their hopes up." *Which is exactly what I did.*

"I don't care. There's a mistake. Your name should be on that list. I'm going in there right now and ask Coach Parks why you didn't make the team."

Mack grabbed Ashley's arm. "No. Don't go in there. It's okay. I'll just . . . I'll just play soccer and try out again next year."

Ashley lifted her eyebrows. "Are you coming with me or not?"

"C'mon, Ashley. Don't."

Ashley wrestled her arm free and was just about to knock on the girls' P.E. office door when it opened.

Mack took a step back when Coach Parks walked out.

Coach Parks smiled. "Well, hello girls. Are you excited about practice this afternoon?"

Mack was shocked into silence. How could Coach Parks make such a cruel joke? What was it? Be mean to Mack day or something?

Ashley cleared her throat. "Coach?"

"Yes?"

"I was just going to, um, ask you about Mack."

"Oh?" Coach Parks looked at Mack. "What about her?"

"Um, I think maybe she should have made the team instead of me."

Mack cringed and tried to find some way to melt into the concrete floor.

"Instead of? What are you—?" Coach Parks turned to look at the list. "Oh, no. Mackenzie, I am so sorry. I left your name off the list."

"What?" Mack and Ashley asked together.

Coach Parks pulled the list off the bulletin board. "I see what happened. Look here." She pointed to the names. "See how the numbers jump from six to eight? I bet you were number seven. C'mon, let's go in the office and check this out."

They followed their coach into her office and stood just inside the doorway. Mack felt really weird. Kids only went into a teacher's office or up to a teacher's desk when they got in trouble.

Coach Parks rustled through some papers on her desk. "Look, here's my handwritten list. Number six is Halie Henri and number seven is Mackenzie Kelly. I guess I'm no good at this computer spreadsheet stuff. I was trying to modernize."

"That's okay, Coach." Mack felt her insides scrunch up. She didn't really mind that her coach had trouble with computers. She was stoked that she'd actually made the team and was going to play softball every single day.

Coach Parks smiled. "Practice is at three-thirty as usual. Bring sweats today because we're sliding."

Mack and Ashley turned to leave.

"Oh, and Mack?" Coach Parks said.

"Yeah?"

"Thanks for being so forgiving. I'd hate to give my new starting center fielder a heart attack on the first day."

Mack's mouth dropped open. "Starting center field?"

"If you're willing."

Mack swallowed hard. "Okay."

"See you at practice, girls."

Mack grabbed Ashley's arm, and they squealed all the way out of the office.

"Guess what?" Ashley shrieked.

"What?"

"Bag o' Chips doesn't know."

"Doesn't know what?"

"Halie doesn't know you made the team, dude. I can't wait to see the look on her face when you show up at practice today."

Mack's smile almost cracked her face it was so big.

Chapter 4

Practice

After school, Mack and Ashley waited for Halie to make her way toward the practice field before they dashed into the locker room to change.

"Hurry up," Mack squealed. "We can't be late for our first-ever practice."

"I know. I know. I'm hurrying. Where'd I put my socks?"

"Right there, right there." Mack pointed then pulled up her own socks. She threw on her cleats and tied them up as quickly as she could. She stashed her backpack in her P.E. locker and checked her softball bag for her glove, visor, sweats, and sunglasses. She had to have sunglasses. Florida wasn't called the Sunshine State for nothing, and she'd need them in center field. Maybe she should ask for flip-up sunglasses for her birthday. Jessica Mendoza probably had flip-up sunglasses.

"C'mon, dude. What are you doing?"

"Sorry. I'm coming." Mack slammed her locker shut and ran after Ashley. She couldn't wait to see the look on Halie's face when she walked into the dugout.

They hustled toward the field and then snuck along the outside of the cinderblock dugout.

Ashley put out a hand to stop Mack. "Okay," she whispered. "Just act natural, as if nothing's wrong. Let's talk about *American Idol* or something."

"Okay." Mack did her best to suppress the giggles threatening to burst free as they opened the gate to the field.

"So what did you think about that singer last night? He was bad, wasn't he?" Ashley said coolly.

Mack struggled to keep the smile off her face. "Yeah, and his hair was way weird."

"Way too much gel."

With a boldness she didn't know she had, Mack plopped her bag on the team bench right next to Halie, and said, "Oh, hey Halie," as if they did that every day. She opened her bag and pulled out her glove and hair band. With both hands, she pulled her long black hair into a ponytail and threw the elastic band around it.

"Huh?" Halie said in a surprised voice. Mack held in a grin at her confused expression. "What the—?"

Mack put a hand over her mouth to hide her smile. Ashley tried unsuccessfully to hold in her giggles.

"What are you doing here?" Halie demanded, a hand on her hip.

"It's time for practice."

"You didn't make the team."

"Yeah, actually, she did," Ashley said from behind Mack. "Coach put up the real list right after you left. Too bad your name was still on it."

Mack spun around wide-eyed, and Ashley giggled uncontrollably.

They grabbed their gloves and ran out to the field to start their warm-up throws. "Oh, my God, dude. We are such dead meat now."

"I know," Mack squealed and threw the yellow ball to Ashley.

Ashley caught the ball and threw it back. "That was, like, the best."

"Well, I'm not going to let her get to me anymore. I know I can play softball, and I have a right to be here just like she does. And, you know what?"

"What?"

"Someday when we're in the College World Series, I'm going to hit a walk-off home run against Halie, and *my* team will be the world champions, not *hers*."

"Sounds good to me. We're both going to play for Florida State, right?"

"I'm going to the University of Texas. You know that. I'm going to be a Longhorn." She held her hand up with her pinky and index finger extended in the Longhorn hand signal.

"You should come to FSU with me." Ashley made a tomahawk chop with her arm.

"Florida State's got a good softball team, don't they?"

"Of course they do."

"I wonder if FSU ever plays Texas." Mack moved under the pop Ashley threw to her. "Oh, my God, Ash. Can you imagine us playing against each other in college?"

"That would be so cool, dude. Hey, throw me some grounders." Ashley squatted in her ready position. "I'd have to console you, though, when my Seminoles kicked your Longhorn butt."

"No way. It'll be your sorry Seminole butt that'll be sobbing because we mercy ruled you."

"No way, dude."

"Yes way." Mack tossed her another grounder. "Second basemen always want grounders."

"Oh, yeah? Well, center fielders always want pops." Ashley threw another sky high pop.

Mack moved under the towering pop and caught it easily. Just as she was about to throw Ashley another grounder, Coach Parks called the team together.

The butterflies that Mack thought she had under control sprang to life as the team gathered around Coach Parks. She made sure she stood as far away from the big old Bag of Chips and her Chipettes as possible. It didn't do any good. Halie glared at her the whole time.

Chapter 5

Stick Together

Mack had no idea so much softball could be crammed into one practice, and they still had a half hour to go. A lot of the girls, the eighth graders especially, had been on the team before so they already knew Coach Parks's drills, but Mack did her best to keep up.

Taylor Rothman, the team's left fielder, helped Mack get the hang of things. Taylor was at least six inches taller than her own five foot two, but she didn't let Taylor's size intimidate her, because after all, Taylor was almost in high school. Besides Coach Parks, Taylor was the only girl on the team with short hair. Her light brown hair fell just above the collar of her t-shirt.

"Hey, Rookie," Taylor yelled from left field. "Coach wants us to do a backing up drill while she's working with the infielders."

"Okay, what do I do?" Mack smiled. She already had a nickname.

"Kristina's going to throw a pop to us and we have to decide who's going to get it. If I call it, then you go behind me just in case I miss it, which won't happen, but you never know, right?"

"Yeah." Mack still had that nervous twitter in her stomach. "And you'll back me up when I call it, right?"

"You got it. Okay, Kristina, we're ready."

Kristina Overton was an eighth grader and the team's first-string pitcher. Mack figured out pretty quickly that when the pitchers weren't directly involved in their own drills, Coach made them help out. In fact, Halie was chasing balls behind first base. She smiled a little at the thought of Halie reduced to ball girl.

Kristina nodded. "Okay, here it comes." She threw a high pop toward Mack in center field.

Mack leaped into action even though it was an easy one. She didn't want Coach Parks or Taylor to think she was a slacker or worse, cocky about how she played. "I got it," she yelled nice and loud.

"I got your back," Taylor yelled and scooted about twenty feet behind Mack.

Mack caught the ball and threw it back to Kristina.

"Hey, I know that one was easy, but we still have to practice backing each other up," Taylor said. "Who knows? You could get stung by a bee and miss it."

"Stung by a bee?"

"You never know." Taylor grinned and trotted back to left field. "My turn."

Kristina tossed the ball in Taylor's direction.

"I got your back," Mack shouted as she ran behind the left fielder.

The drill continued for a few more minutes, and Mack was proud that she caught each and every one of the balls that Kristina threw her—even the ones that were kind of hard to reach. Taylor missed two, and Mack wasn't sure, but thought maybe Taylor missed them on purpose to make sure she knew how to back up. She didn't really care, she was just happy to be on the team.

"Bring it in, girls," Coach Parks yelled from behind the plate. "Okay, we've got about twenty minutes left. I want to do a full field drill for ten minutes and a quick sliding lesson after that. Outfielders, I'll call out the base I want you to throw to. You need to call every ball and make sure you back each other up like you just practiced."

After Coach Parks gave instructions to the infielders, Mack ran back out to center field. She crouched down in the ready position and waited.

"Second base," Coach Parks yelled and hit an easy fly ball to Taylor in left field. Mack trotted behind her, just in case Taylor got stung by a bee. As expected, Taylor caught the ball easily and threw it to Ashley at second base.

Mack ran back to her position in center and took a quick millisecond to smile. It looked liked Ashley might be the starting second baseman. That was so cool. Too bad Halie would only be the second string pitcher. Ha-ha.

"Second base," Coach yelled again and hit a pop up to Mack in center.

"I got it," Mack yelled and caught the ball easily. She tossed it to Ashley who smiled big at her.

The drill progressed, and Coach Parks hit the ball in between the outfielders and not directly at them. Mack, Taylor, and Marci, the right fielder, had to run in or back or to the side for them. Mack understood why it was so important to call the ball, because sometimes she and Taylor ran toward the ball and, if no one called for it, they would collide for sure. Colliding with the big eighth grader wouldn't be fun.

"Coming home," Coach Parks yelled as she hit the ball in between Taylor and Mack.

Mack could have gotten to the ball, but since Taylor was an eighth grader and a lot more experienced, she decided to let her have it. "Yours, yours. I got your back."

Taylor missed the ball by a good two feet, so Mack scurried after it and threw it with all her might to Beth, the shortstop, who turned and tossed it to Stephanie at home plate.

"Mackenzie Kelly." Coach Parks pointed at Mack with her bat.

Mack stopped in her tracks. "Yes, ma'am?" Coach Parks sounded really mad.

"Are you the center fielder?"

"Yes, ma'am."

"Then you're in charge out there. Any ball you can get to is yours. Taylor and Marci will back you up. Is that clear?"

"Any ball?"

"Any and every ball. If it's in your reach, then get it."

Mack swallowed hard. "Okay," she called back in a high, tight voice. She didn't want to be a ball hog, but Coach told her to go for everything.

"Okay, let's do that one again. Going home."

Coach Parks smashed the ball in between Mack and Taylor in about the same place she'd hit the last one.

Mack knew she could get it. "I got it. I got it." On the run, she snatched the ball out of the air and then whipped it to Beth.

Beth relayed the ball home, and Coach Parks yelled, "That's it, Mackenzie. That's exactly what a center fielder does. Good job. Bring it in girls. It's time for a quick lesson on sliding."

The outfielders ran in, and Taylor high-fived Mack. "Rookie, you're fast. I couldn't reach those last ones. Coach is right, you know. If you can get 'em, go for it. I'll be happy to back you up any day."

"Me, too," Marci said and joined them on their way in. "Outfielders have to stick together."

"Stick together?" Taylor put her fist out.

Mack knocked fists with Taylor and then with Marci. "Stick together."

Chapter 6

2016

Mack loved Friday nights because they were cheat nights, and her mom usually ordered pizza or Chinese or even made macaroni and cheese from a box. But she also loved Friday nights because those stupid English tests were over for another week. She never understood why Mrs. Hendricks had to have a test every single stupid Friday.

Her dad handed her another slice of pepperoni pizza.

"Thanks." People always said she looked like her dad. And, yeah, she did kind of have his dark wavy hair and brown eyes while her mom had thin light brown hair and blue eyes. She definitely had her dad's straight nose, too, but other than that, she thought she just kind of looked like herself.

"Hey, Stinky, why so quiet?" her dad asked.

"I don't know." She reached for her glass of milk and saw her parents exchange a look. Oh, no, Mrs. Hendricks must have called home again.

Her mom was the accountant for a whole mess of doctors and dentists in Central Florida and her dad was the business manager for PDC Electronics in Orlando. Both had Masters' degrees in business and probably wondered why their one offspring couldn't manage to pass sixth grade English.

Mack couldn't figure it out either because she had really studied for that stupid English test. She read the story over and over again and thought she understood everything. She had run out of time. Again. She prayed her parents wouldn't bring up Mrs. Hendricks or English and ruin a perfectly good cheat night dinner.

"Hey, what do you want for your birthday?" her mom asked. She was obviously trying to move to a happy topic.

Mack looked up from her pizza. "Oh, c'mon. You guys know what I want."

Her parents laughed, and her dad rolled his eyes. "Go ahead and remind us, Stinky."

"Do you have to call me that?"

"Hey, your mom made me change your diapers when you were a baby. Phew." He waved a hand in front of his nose.

"Mom." Mack looked at her mom for some sort of rescue.

Her mom simply shrugged. "If the shoe fits . . ."

"You're no help."

"Speaking of shoes," her dad continued, "have you smelled those cleats of yours after practice?"

"Dad." She pretended to throw her slice of pizza at him.

"Okay, okay. I give up." He put his hands up in surrender. "But, seriously, Stinky, besides a Cat Osterman softball glove and anything else with Cat's name on it, what do you want?"

"A Jessica Mendoza bat?"

Her dad laughed. "You have a one track mind. So do you think you'll ever play on the same team with Miss Osterman?"

"Of course," she said matter-of-factly.

"Got this all planned out?"

"Well, yeah, because first we'll be on the Olympic team together and then I'll be her teammate in the National Pro Fastpitch League. They call it the NPF or something. She plays for the Rockford Thunder—that's in Illinois. But first I'll play for the University of Texas like she did."

"What's wrong with the University of Central Florida?" her mom asked. "That's where I met your dad."

"UCF? C'mon. Besides you guys, who ever went there?"

"Oh, lots of people. Like Bob Opsahl, the TV news guy on channel nine. Oh, and Daunte Culpepper for instance."

"The NFL quarterback?"

"Um hmm. And who was that WNBA player who went to UCF, honey?" Her mom directed the question to her dad.

"Oh, right. Um, wait a second. Tari . . . Tari something."

"Phillips. Tari Phillips," her mom finished. "I think you were too young to remember, but she played basketball on the Orlando Miracle when we had a WNBA team here, and she also played with the New York Liberty and the Houston Comets, too."

"Oh, and Miss America," her dad added. "Ericka Dunlap went to UCF."

"That's nice, but I don't want to be Miss America."

"Okay," her mom said, "how about Michelle Akers?"

"The soccer player? From the Olympics?"

"Yeah, from the Olympics."

Mack thought about it for a second. "Okay, they sound cool and all, but who wants to be a Golden Knight when you can be a Texas Longhorn?" She flashed the Longhorn sign to her parents with both hands.

"Obviously, dear," her mom said to her dad, "we need to take this kid to some UCF games."

"I think you're right." He faced Mack again. "Stinky, I hate to burst your bubble, but you know that softball's been taken out of the Olympics. This is the last year."

Mack squirmed in her seat and gazed down at her half-eaten slice of pizza. She tried to keep the disappointment out of her voice. "I know, but maybe by the time I'm on the team they'll get it back. Lots of countries, like China and Australia and Japan, play softball now. That stupid committee—what are they called, Dad?"

"The IOC. The International Olympic Committee."

"Well, that stupid IOC will see how wrong they were and how they made a bad decision for 2012. Besides, in 2012"—she stopped to do the math in her head—"I'll only be in tenth grade. Well, just finished, so that's still kind of young to make the Olympic team, but maybe in 2016 when I'm in college—just before my junior year—"

"At Texas, of course," her dad interrupted with a grin.

Mack made a face at him. "Of course, but, like I was saying before I was so rudely interrupted, they'll get the Olympics back just in time for me and Cat Osterman to play on the same team."

"And Jessica Mendoza?"

Mack sat up taller. "Yeah, she'll play left field and I'll play center."

"Where's Caitlin Lowe going to play?" her dad asked.

"Oh. I didn't think about that."

"I guess you have some time to work that out," her mom said.

Mack felt her heart get heavy, and a sad silence overcame her.

"What can we do to get softball back in the Olympics?"

Her mom sighed. "I don't know. Maybe we can search the Internet for more information."

Mack beamed. "Yeah, everything's on the net. Ashley has this phone with the internet on it." She stopped when she remembered what she really wanted for her birthday. "Hey, can I get a cell phone?"

"No," her dad answered, "we've been over this. You're too young. Maybe when you're a teenager."

"Oh," Mack groaned. "A whole 'nother year? But everybody's texting now, and I'm the only one in the whole world without texting." She sighed loud enough for her parents to hear. *I bet Cat Osterman has texting.*

She pushed her chair back, leaving her second slice of pizza half-eaten. "Can I be excused?"

Her parents exchanged another meaningful look even though Mack had no idea what it meant.

"Yes," her mom said. "Put your plate and milk glass in the sink, please."

Mack put her dishes in the sink and then turned on the backyard floodlights so she could throw pop flies to herself. It wasn't the texting thing that had gotten her upset. It was the Olympics.

She threw the ball high in the air and almost hit the top of her mom's palm tree. How could the stupid IOC make such a stupid decision? The Olympics without softball would be like Florida without palm trees.

She thought and thought as she threw the ball higher and higher into the dark Florida sky, but she couldn't figure out what she, an almost twelve-year-old girl who was too young for a cell phone, could do to get softball back for the 2016 Olympics.

Chapter 7

Evil Mrs. Hendricks

As much as Mack loved Friday nights, that's how much she hated Mondays. Well, Monday mornings fourth period, anyway, because that's when Mrs. Hendricks usually passed back the tests they'd taken on Friday. Mack rarely got a good grade on those things, and she hated being shown proof of how dumb she was.

With about five minutes left in class, Mrs. Hendricks picked up the stack of tests from her desk and handed them out so slowly that Mack wanted to scream. Halie got her test back and showed everyone, including Mack, that she had gotten an A-plus. Mack looked away and waited for the inevitable. She wondered if she would get another gentleman's D or a fabulously fashionable F.

"Okay, everyone," Mrs. Hendricks said from the front of the room, "we ran a little long today, so we'll go over your tests tomorrow. For homework, please read the story starting on page 112 in your text."

Mack raised her hand.

"Yes, Mackenzie?"

"I didn't get my test back."

"Oh, yes, I know." Mrs. Hendricks sat down at her desk and rifled through the top desk drawer.

Mack looked down at her hands folded on her desk. She hoped Mrs. Hendricks hadn't lost her test because she definitely didn't want to have to take it again. She heard Halie and her friends whispering behind her, but she did her best to ignore them.

"Well, Mackenzie?" Mrs. Hendricks called in her impatient way. "Do you want your test or not?"

Mack stood up quickly and scooted to the front as fast as she could. She stood next to Mrs. Hendricks with her arms folded. She cringed when she heard Halie singsong to her friends, "Uh, oh. Mack's in trouble again."

The bell rang and the students headed out the door.

"Let's wait for the other students to leave, shall we?" Mrs. Hendricks said.

Halie huddled with her little friends near the classroom door and then they all turned around at once, looked at Mack, and burst out laughing.

Mack did her best to turn invisible, but couldn't so she stared at the floor and shifted her weight from one foot to the other. She knew she was turning red, because she felt her cheeks getting hot. Why did Mrs. Hendricks torture her like this?

Mack decided to move things along. "Did you find my test, ma'am?" Her insides shook, and she clenched her jaw so tightly it hurt.

Mrs. Hendricks pulled out her red grade book. Most of Mack's other teachers used a computer to keep track of grades, but not Mrs. Hendricks. She still recorded her grades with pencil and paper. Mrs. Hendricks opened her grade book and pulled out the test. Mack gulped when she saw a Post-It note with her home phone number stuck to it. She had been right. Mrs. Hendricks did call home last Friday.

Slowly, as if pulling a band aid off a cut, Mrs. Hendricks peeled off the Post-It note and then flopped the test on her desk face up. Mack stared at the big fat F with a thick red circle around it. Scrawled on the side were the words, "See me."

"Mackenzie, I want you to look at all this red on your test. I practically used up an entire grading pen on it."

Mack wasn't sure if she was supposed to apologize, but she really felt no sympathy for Mrs. Hendricks's ink supply.

"First of all," Mrs. Hendricks continued, "your handwriting is atrocious, and you've made so many careless mistakes I couldn't keep track. You shouldn't be making mistakes like these at your age, especially with spelling." She scanned the first page. "Ah, here's a good example. See how you wrote d-o-s-e instead of d-o-*e*-*s*? And look at this one. You spelled it c-u-a-g-h-t instead of c-*a*-*u*-g-h-t? I mean, really. What were you thinking? Or maybe you weren't. And," she flipped the test to the back page, "you didn't finish."

"I know. The bell rang, and I wasn't done."

"Mackenzie Kelly," she said in that fed-up tone that Mack had gotten used to over the past five months. "If everyone else managed to finish the test on time, why couldn't you? You are just going to have to try harder. Work faster."

Mack had no response. What she wanted to say was that when she did try to finish a test on time, she got all the answers wrong and failed. And when she tried to slow down and get correct answers, she always ran out of time and still failed. Mrs. Hendricks would never ever let her have more time, so she just stood there quietly, wishing she could leave.

"How do you expect to get into college, Mackenzie? Your parents must be so disappointed." Mrs. Hendricks sighed. "I've contacted your guidance counselor and your parents about your poor grades. With your lazy approach to studying, I just might recommend you not be rewarded with playing that time-wasting baseball after school. You should be putting your time to better use, young lady."

Mack knew she stared rudely as Mrs. Hendricks wrote the hall pass. But how could Mrs. Hendricks, evil Mrs. Hendricks, take away the one thing that helped her stay sane? And she didn't even know enough to call it softball. She was almost as mean as that stupid committee that took softball out of the Olympics.

Mack took the hall pass and then shoved her stupid test into her backpack. She wanted to bolt from the classroom, but forced herself to walk slowly and calmly out the door. It was probably the hardest thing she'd ever done in her entire life.

Chapter 8

The Signs

Mack stood shoulder to shoulder with the other outfielders. She put her hand on top of Taylor's in the middle of their human circle.

Taylor looked them all in the eye. "On three. One, two, three."

"Stick together," they yelled and ran to their respective positions.

Halie was their outfield driller that day. Mack took a deep breath and wondered what joys the old Bag of Chips would bring to her world.

"Coach wants us to do blind pops," Halie called to the outfielders.

Mack groaned. The blind pop drill was kind of scary. Kristina had done the drill with them once before, but only for, like, two minutes.

One by one the three outfielders turned away from Halie and faced the outfield fence.

"It's up," Halie yelled.

Mack turned around quickly and looked to the sky for the pop. It was in left field. Taylor's ball. "Taylor. Yours, yours."

Taylor had trouble finding it, and the ball fell to the ground. Mack picked up the ball and tossed it back in to Halie.

Taylor took off her glove. "Hang on a second, Henry."

"My last name is spelled H-e-n-r-i and it's pronounced 'On-Ree.' It's French. Not 'Hen-Ree.'" Halie looked as if she'd never been more insulted in her life.

"Okay, sorry. Anyway, Rookie, c'mere."

Mack headed toward Taylor in left field. "What's up?"

"I couldn't find the stupid ball. We have to help each other, so if it's my ball, just tell me to go left or right, in or back."

"Left or right. In or back," Mack repeated to make sure she understood. "Okay."

Taylor reminded Marci and the other outfielders about helping each other, and they were ready for the second throw from Halie. Once again, they turned away and faced the fence.

"It's up," Halie yelled.

Mack looked up, but didn't see the ball.

"Mack, it's yours. Left. Left."

Mack took several steps toward left field, but she still didn't see the ball. She groaned when it hit the ground near Marci in right field. Halie burst out laughing.

"You said 'left,'" Mack complained to Taylor.

"I did," Taylor said, "and you went to your right."

"No, I went toward you in left field."

"Which is to your right."

Mack realized her error. "Oh."

Once Halie collected herself, they tried the drill again, and once again Mack went the wrong direction. She threw her glove on the ground. "I can't get this."

Taylor ran over to her in center field. Marci, along with the rest of the outfielders, joined them.

"Okay. Okay. Here's what we'll do," Taylor said. "If it's closer to me then I'll yell something like, 'school, school' since the school is on my side of the field. If it's in the right field direction, then we'll yell 'street, street.' No more left and right. Does that sound okay?"

"Okay, I guess." Mack wasn't sure Coach Parks would like this new way of communicating.

"But we all have to do it this way," Marci added, "because I'm not going to remember when to say what."

"Cool," Taylor said. "And when we play at other schools we'll figure out new signals."

"Agreed." Mack put her hand in the outfielders' circle.

Taylor smiled. "On three. One, two, three."

"Stick together!"

Mack had much more success with Taylor's new system and after about ten more minutes of the drill, Coach Parks called the entire team to the dugout.

"Have a seat on the bench, girls. We're already into our third week of practice, and it's time to learn the signs."

A few of the girls groaned, but Mack didn't know what was happening. Ashley shrugged as if she didn't know what was going on either.

"Oh, c'mon now," Coach Parks reprimanded playfully. "Reading signs isn't that hard. In fact, we'll start off easy. In this first round, I won't give you the indicator. Let's just say that I've already hit the indicator and the sign is on."

Mack looked wide-eyed at Ashley who'd become equally wide-eyed. She hoped that Coach Parks would tell them what the heck an indicator was because reading signs was confusing already.

"Okay, girls. I'll flash you a lot of signs, but when I hit my right elbow, it means bunt. When I hit my left knee that means steal."

Coach Parks whirled around and pointed at Taylor. "So if the left knee means steal, what does hit the right knee mean?"

Taylor looked confident. "It means nothing. Well, except to hit away."

"Excellent. Okay, everybody ready?"

Mack didn't outwardly move her head, but inwardly she shook her head so fast she gave herself an imaginary headache.

Coach Parks touched her chin, hip, back of her hand, top of her head, belt buckle, knee, and nose.

"Halie?"

"Oh, uh, steal."

Mack felt as lost as the time she got turned around in the Altamonte Mall in fourth grade. She couldn't find her mom then, and she had no idea what was happening now.

"Yes, Halie. Good," Coach Parks said. "I touched my left knee. I touched a lot of other things, too, but those are meaningless. Here we go, let's do this again." Coach Parks moved both hands this time and touched a lot of the same things, but she touched an elbow this time. Elbow meant bunt.

"Mack?"

"Bunt."

"Nope. Ashley, why isn't it bunt?"

"Because you touched your right elbow, not your left."

"Good. Do you see that now, Mack?"

"Yeah." *But what I really mean is, "No."*

Coach Parks ran through the signs a few more times and during the last go around she called on Mack again.

Okay, Mack thought, *I've gotten most of these wrong, but she touched her knee and knee means steal.* "Steal," she announced with confidence.

Halie and her Chipettes burst out laughing.

"Girls," Coach admonished. "C'mon now. We're all still learning." Halie covered her mouth with a hand, but Mack could see her shoulders shaking as she laughed.

"Okay, grab your gear and head on back to the gym. Looks like we've got a Florida rainstorm coming in so we might as well get our uniforms today."

Mack watched the dark clouds move swiftly toward them. She sighed. She had no idea how she was going to learn all those signs.

"I hope I get number three," Ashley said excitedly.

"C'mon, we'd better run because the rain's almost here." Mack threw her glove in her bag and picked it up.

The black rain clouds were as dark and miserable as she felt. The only silver lining to the practice might be if she could get number eight on her jersey.

She and Ashley headed toward the open doorway of the dugout, but Coach stopped her.

"Mack, can I have a word?" Before Mack could answer, Coach Parks said to Taylor, "Thank you for sharing that with me. You and Ashley had better hurry before the rain gets you."

"See you later, dude." Ashley hustled out of the dugout and ran toward the gym.

Big fat rain drops smacked the ground.

"Oops, I guess we're stuck in here for a few minutes, but, hey, this gives us time to work out those signs. You had some trouble, didn't you?"

"I'm sorry, ma'am."

"That's all right. Now, first of all," she said with a smile to let Mack know she wasn't angry, "could you please stop calling me ma'am? It makes me think my mom's here."

"Okay, sorry."

"Oh, don't be sorry. But listen, reading signs can be tricky. I've got a plan. How about you and I work out a different set of signs. Nobody else needs to know what we're doing. It'll be our secret, okay?"

"Okay. What do I have to do?"

"If I hit my belt that means bunt. B for bunt."

"Okay, easy."

"Steal, steal, steal. What can I—oh, shoulder. If I touch my shoulder that means steal."

"S for steal. Got it. Test me. Quick." She had this. Too bad Halie and Ashley and Taylor weren't there to see it.

Coach flashed what seemed like a thousand signs, but finally touched her belt.

"Bunt."

"You got it, kiddo."

Coach Parks ran through as many rounds of signs as the quickly moving rain storm allowed. "A-plus, kiddo. I think you've got it now. See, reading the signs isn't so hard after all, is it?"

Mack shook her head, pleased that her coach let her have a second chance. She hoped Mrs. Hendricks let her have another chance, too.

Chapter 9

Happy Birthday to Me

Mack took a huge breath and blew out the candles with one mighty blast. She made her wish, the one she'd been making ever since she'd discovered softball. She wished she would someday play on the Olympic softball team. She didn't know if she was allowed to, but she made a second wish. This one was for better grades in English.

Her parents and Ashley clapped as she took out the now smoldering candles one by one.

"Let me help." Ashley pulled out one of the waxy candles. She licked off the chocolate frosting and put it on the napkin with the others. "You have to open my present first."

Mack looked at her mom.

"Sure, girls, but Mack has to cut the first slice of cake before she does that. For good luck."

Good luck. Yeah, she could use some good luck about now. She was bummed that her birthday fell on a school night with Mrs. Hendricks's stupid weekly test the very next day. *Happy birthday to me.*

Ever since Mrs. Hendricks chewed her out and threatened to take her off the team, Mack studied English every single night. She had even gotten a D-plus on the very next test. It wasn't great, but at least it showed improvement. Mack wasn't sure if a D-plus was a real grade, because it kind of meant "poor plus" which was almost insulting, but at least it wasn't an F.

Mack cut the first slice of cake and set it down in front of herself. Chocolate cake with chocolate frosting. Yum, her favorite. She took a bite and as soon as she put her fork down, Ashley shoved a box in front of her.

"Open it. My dad picked it out."

"Your dad?"

"Yeah, just open it."

Mack ripped off the dark red wrapping paper and yellow ribbon. She opened the box and laughed. She pulled out a red and gold Florida State University visor and plunked it on her head.

"See, dude," Ashley said, "now you're all set to go to FSU with me."

Mack didn't want to go to FSU any more than she wanted to go to UCF. She wanted to go to the University of Texas and everybody knew it. She did her best to be polite. "Thanks, Ash."

"No problem, dude."

Her mom placed a piece of birthday cake in front of Ashley.

"Oh, thanks, Mrs. Kelly."

"Mmm hmm." Mack's mom served her husband and then herself some cake.

"Here, Stinky." Her dad pushed a large box toward her on the floor. "Open this one next."

"Is it a cell phone?"

Her dad smiled, but shook his head.

She ripped open the purple paper and pulled up the top flaps of the box. She groaned when she saw another wrapped box inside. "Dad, c'mon."

Her parents laughed.

"Hey, a little hard work never hurt anybody," her mom said.

Why does everybody keep telling me that? Mack sighed and tried to ignore the fact that after she opened presents, she had to go to her room and study for an English test. On her birthday. That was just wrong.

Mack lifted up the package and saw a lot more presents underneath. "Oh, cool."

Ashley looked in the box, and her eyes grew big. "Dude, you're cleaning up."

Mack grinned and tore the paper off the present. She stood up, knocking her chair over. "No way. A Cat Osterman glove? You found a lefty one? How cool. Thanks, Mom. Thanks, Dad." She gave each of her parents a hug and then reverently slipped the signature glove on her hand. She opened and closed the glove a few times. "It's pretty broken in already."

"Daddy worked on that thing every night after you went to bed."

"You did?" She looked at her dad.

He let out an exaggerated sigh. "Yes, but it's your job from now on."

"Okay."

"Dude, let me see that." Ashley grabbed for the glove. Mack was hesitant to take it off her hand, but she had a boxful of other presents to open. She handed Ashley the glove, up-righted her chair, and was about to pick out another present, when her mom handed her a long narrow package.

"Here, honey, open this one next. It wouldn't fit in the box."

Mack ripped off the paper and squeezed her hands around a brand new Jessica Mendoza bat.

"Dude," Ashley said, eyeing the bat. "You're going to let me use that, aren't you?"

Mack took a careful quarter swing. "As long as you don't hurt it." She held the bat up high and smiled.

Her mom held out a hand. "Let me put that over here so you don't hit a home run with the chandelier." She placed the bat in the corner of the dining room.

Mack opened the next present to reveal a red, white, and blue Olympic Team USA visor. "How cool." She ripped off the FSU visor and snuggled the Olympic team one on her head. "This will go great with my number eight jersey at school, but someday I'm going to wear one of these visors for real."

"Me, too." Ashley and Mack knocked fists.

Mack opened her next gift—a black University of Central Florida visor and gold t-shirt with black lettering. Mack said a polite thank you and reluctantly pulled off the Team USA visor to put on the UCF one.

"And," her dad said, pulling an envelope from his shirt pocket, "we're going to a UCF softball game next Saturday."

"We are? Can Ashley come?"

Her dad laughed. "You two are joined at the hip, aren't you? Yes, we got a ticket for her, too. UCF has a tournament, so we'll see two games."

Mack adjusted the UCF visor on her head. She felt bad that she had dismissed the school so quickly. She'd wear her new UCF stuff when they went to the games.

The next gift surprised her.

"Stanford?" She held up the red visor and red t-shirt.

"Mmm hmm." Her mom nodded. "That's where Jessica Mendoza went to college. Daddy and I thought maybe you needed to keep your options open."

"Cool." Off came the UCF visor, on went Stanford. "Where is Stanford, anyway?"

"California."

California? Mack hadn't considered going so far from home. Austin, Texas was far enough. "I've got a lot of choices now, don't I?"

"Keep going," her dad said and pointed at the remaining presents.

Mack laughed when she pulled out an orange and blue University of Florida visor and t-shirt. "Gators?"

Ashley gasped and started chanting the Seminole war cry as she tomahawk chopped at Mack's new Gator visor.

"Oh, yeah?" Mack put both arms in front of her and Gator chomped Ashley's imaginary tomahawk.

"Ashley's dad told us about the FSU stuff," her dad said, "so we had to get you some Gator stuff. Equal time, you know?"

Ashley stopped chopping. "Mr. Kelly, how could you? Wait 'til my dad hears about this. Dude," she turned to Mack, "this is so warped."

Mack laughed and took off the Stanford visor so she could put on the Gator one. And even though she had no allegiance whatsoever to the University of Florida, she stuck her tongue out at Ashley in triumph.

"Oh, shut up." Ashley put on Mack's discarded FSU visor.

Mack ignored her and pulled out another gift. She hoped, hoped, hoped it would be the visor she really wanted. She slowly tore off the paper. She wanted to prolong the moment. She peeked into the box and saw the coveted orangey mud color. "Yes." She punched a fist in the air.

She practically ripped her hair out in her hurry to remove the Gator visor. She smoothed her hair back down and carefully placed the University of Texas visor on her head as if she were putting on a crown. She grabbed her Cat Osterman glove back from Ashley. "Do I look like a Longhorn?"

Her mom beamed, but her dad said, "Do you even know what a longhorn is, honey?"

"Um, no. What is it?"

"A breed of cattle."

"Cattle? Like as in cows?"

Ashley almost fell out of her chair laughing. "Dude, you're a cow." She smacked the table with her hand.

"C'mon. Really? A longhorn is a cow?" Then it dawned on her. She remembered the picture of the cow with the long horns when she was searching for stuff about Cat Osterman on the Internet.

Her dad nodded and smiled.

"What's Stanford?"

"The Cardinal," her dad answered.

"A red bird?"

He nodded.

Mack sighed. "I don't know." She picked up the University of Florida visor again. "Maybe being a Gator wouldn't be so bad."

"'Noles," Ashley shouted and did the tomahawk chop again.

"Gators." Mack Gator chomped Ashley with the Cat Osterman glove still on her hand.

Her mom shrugged and said to her dad, "We've created a twelve-year-old nightmare, honey."

Chapter 10

Jack Rabbit

Mack whipped off her University of Texas visor and plunked her batting helmet on her head. She picked up her brand new Jessica Mendoza bat and took a few practice swings in the on-deck circle. Halie was pitching batting practice today instead of Kristina who was working with some pitching coach guy that came to practice sometimes.

Mack watched as Taylor took her swings against Halie. She hated to admit it, but Halie was kind of a good pitcher. She cringed when Taylor swung way too early and completely missed Halie's change-up.

"Henry, you're killing me with that pitch. Cut it out," Taylor yelled.

"It's 'On-Ree'—" Halie protested.

"Yeah, yeah, I know, but I get to call you Henry because you keep making me swing and miss."

Mack finally had a chance to laugh at Halie, but she did it quietly. She remembered how it felt to be laughed at and, even if it was the old Bag of Chips, she decided she didn't want to make anyone else feel that rotten.

Mack covered her smile when Taylor swung and missed again. She couldn't understand why Taylor didn't know when Halie was going to throw the change-up. It was so obvious. Halie fumbled with the ball in her glove, held her pitching elbow toward third base instead of center field, and slowed down her delivery toward home plate.

"Okay, Mack," Coach Parks called. "You're up. Ten good swings and then it's slapping practice for you."

"Slapping? Like Natasha Watley?"

Coach Parks laughed. "One can only hope you can slap like Natasha Watley." She chuckled again. "Okay. Only good pitches now. Ten swings."

Mack adjusted her batting helmet and got set in the box for left-handed hitters. Deep ruts scarred the right-handed box where all the other batters dug in their cleats, but the lefty box was smooth and flat because nobody used it, except for her.

Okay, Halie, Mack thought, *just don't throw one at my head.* She watched Halie grip the ball. Nope, not a change-up. The fast ball came right down the middle of the plate, and Mack exploded with her brand new Mendoza bat. The line drive screamed into right field and bounced its way to the fence. Marci threw the ball back in. Mack stopped smiling when she saw Halie's scowl. She took a deep breath and waited for the next pitch.

Halie fumbled with the ball in her glove. Her elbow pointed toward third base. Mack waited for the change-up she knew was coming and hit a long fly ball well over Marci's head. It hit the fence on two hops. She enjoyed watching her new friend's dark braid bounce back and forth as she chased after the monster hit.

Halie tried to fool Mack with her pitches, but Mack smacked each one right back onto the field with authority.

"Great hitting, Mackenzie," Coach Parks said as she called the team together. "You've got a sharp eye up there."

"Thanks, ma'am—I mean, thanks, Coach."

Coach Parks smiled and outlined the next half hour of practice. A lot of the girls, Taylor included, went to the outfield to work on pops and grounders, but Ashley and Mack and Marci and a few others stayed near the plate to learn about slapping.

"You don't see slapping in baseball much, it's kind of unique to softball," Coach Parks began. "Here's the idea. You all know how to sacrifice bunt, but today we're going to incorporate slapping and bunting for a hit into your growing repertoire."

Ashley raised her hand.

"Yes, Ashley?"

"What's a 'repper-twar'?"

Coach Parks laughed. "It's, um, like a collection of things. Like a tool box. We'll be adding new tools to your softball toolbox. Okay, here's what you need to do." Coach Parks stepped into the lefty box, Mack's box.

Ashley's hand shot up again.

"Yes, Ashley?"

"I'm not a lefty."

"You're all lefties when you slap."

Mack almost laughed at how wide Ashley's eyes got, but she was ecstatic. Here was something in her life that might finally give her an advantage over other people. That never happened. Ever.

"Watch me, girls. Take your usual stance. We don't want the other team to suspect anything. Now, slide your front foot back. Your back foot steps forward fast. At this point, I've turned my whole body toward the pitcher and my bat is down ready to bunt. You have two options though—bunt for a hit or slap. Here's the bunt for a hit. Halie, throw me a fast ball right down the middle of the plate, please."

Coach Parks set down a bunt for a hit and ran a couple of steps up the line toward first base. "See how easy that was?"

"Yeah, right," Ashley said under her breath. Mack tried not to smile.

"Let's go through a couple of rounds of bunting for a hit from the lefty box. Go ahead and run it out to first base so the infielders get some practice, too."

Mack stepped up to the plate to take her turn. She hit the ball a little too hard and the first baseman fielded it quickly. Mack exploded out of the box and turned on the speed. She made believe she was Natasha Watley running to first in the gold medal game.

"Safe," somebody yelled.

"How did she do that?" someone else asked.

"Rookie," Taylor called from the outfield. "You're a jack rabbit. Whoo-hoo."

Mack shook her head at the crazy left fielder. She got back in line at the plate, and the others clapped her on the back in amazement.

"Dude, I knew you were fast, but holy wow," Ashley said. "You should be on the track team."

Mack felt her face flush and let herself take pride in something, finally something she could do well.

"Nice job, Mack." Coach Parks picked up Mack's bat. "Okay girls, here's how slapping is different than bunting for a hit. If the third and first basemen think you're going to bunt, they'll come in, usually way in." She gestured for the third and first basemen to move in. "See how close to home they are? This time we're going to slap it past them, just out of their reach. Halie? Another fast ball, please."

Coach Parks looked as if she was going to bunt for a hit again, but then at the last second, took a kind of half swing and punched the ball past the first baseman for a clean base hit.

Mack couldn't believe how simple that looked. She couldn't wait to try.

"All right, girls. We'll try a few rounds without defense to get the hang of it and then we'll get the whole infield back to see if they can get you out."

Mack couldn't understand why the other girls had so much trouble. It was pretty easy.

"I can't do this." Ashley groaned. "Why are you so good at this, dude?"

"Probably 'cuz I'm a natural lefty."

"Maybe, but I don't think I could do this even if I was a lefty."

Coach Parks called the infielders back to their positions. She instructed Halie to continue throwing fast balls and nothing else.

Most of the other girls got their feet so tangled up they couldn't make good contact with the ball, but Mack slapped the ball cleanly past the third baseman the first time and then past the first baseman the second time.

The third time Mack got up to bat, she saw Halie switch her grip to the change-up. Halie started her windup, and Mack readied herself. She waited just the right amount of time and slapped the ball up the middle past Halie in the circle. *That'll teach her to mess with me,* she thought smugly.

Coach Parks called an end to the practice shortly after that. Halie slung her bag over her shoulder and said to her Chipettes, "Maybe she can play, but she still can't read."

Chapter 11

Olympic Dreams

Mack sat in her fourth period English class on Monday morning amazed that she was almost looking forward to getting her test back. Friday's test hadn't been that hard. Not really. She hadn't finished it, as usual, but she kind of knew more of the vocabulary words this time. She suspected that all that extra studying she did on her birthday had helped.

She opened her textbook and turned to the story that Mrs. Hendricks wanted the class to read for homework. She liked when teachers let her start homework in class. With softball taking up the entire afternoon before dinner, she liked to get a head start on her homework, but today she was a little antsy. That afternoon they were starting their fourth week of practice which, according to Coach Parks, meant scrimmage time. Since they didn't have enough players for a full team on team scrimmage, five girls would make up the batting team and they'd bat against the other nine players in the field. They'd keep switching things up until everybody had a chance to hit. She couldn't wait.

Mack looked at the clock. Grrr, ten long minutes until lunch. And then P.E. after that, but they were playing flag football which was kind of cool. History would be really boring, but then Science during eighth period would save the day because they were starting a unit on electric circuits. So except for math and science and P.E. and lunch, she just tried to survive the school day until softball.

She looked back up at the clock. Eight more minutes to go. She tapped the desk with her pencil and watched the second hand make its way around the clock face. The story in her textbook sat unread in front of her.

Mrs. Hendricks picked up the stack of tests from her desk. Mack prayed to the gods of partial credit for at least a C on this one. Mrs. Hendricks handed out the tests one by one by one. An ache gnawed at her stomach when she wasn't handed her test.

"Mackenzie?" Mrs. Hendricks called to her quietly.

"Yes, ma'am."

"Come up here, please."

Mack shuffled slowly to the front and prayed that Mrs. Hendricks would tell her that she'd passed and that she was proud of all the hard work she'd put into studying.

"Mackenzie, I've already called your mom, your guidance counselor, and your coach."

Alarm bells rang in Mack's head. *She called Mom? And Coach Parks?*

"I'm sorry," Mrs. Hendricks continued, "but you're off the baseball team until your grades improve. Coach Parks wants to see you after school today. I suspect to turn in your equipment."

Mack's ears were on a five second delay. She didn't understand. Did Mrs. Hendricks just say "off the team"? Off the team meant—

She gasped when realization hit her. "You can't kick me off the team," she blurted. She'd definitely get grounded for being so rude to a teacher, but she didn't care.

"Mackenzie Kelly. I can and I did. Hood Middle School's policy says that if students don't have the grades, they can't play on sports teams."

Mack blinked back the tears that stung her eyes.

"Don't give me that face," Mrs. Hendricks said.

What face? Mack screamed in her head. *The face that says you just destroyed my entire life and my dream of playing softball in the Olympics? My dream to play with Jessica Mendoza in the outfield and to save Cat Osterman's perfect game with a diving catch in center field? My dream of winning the gold medal game by stealing home and having my teammates put me on their shoulders and parade me around the Olympic field? You just shattered my Olympic dreams, so what kind of face do you expect me to have?*

Mack pulled her Team USA visor over her face so no one would see her cry. Even Halie had the decency not to laugh in the tomblike quiet classroom. She slunk back to her seat and put her head down on the desk counting the seconds until her life was over.

Chapter 12

Another Test

Mack knocked on the Girls' Physical Education office door. Coach Parks gestured for her to come in. "I was expecting you."

"Mrs. Hendricks told me to see you." She clasped her hands in front of her and hoped Coach wouldn't see them trembling.

"Mrs. Hendricks told me a little bit about your, uh, troubles in English. I'm going to make a phone call and see what I can do to help. Okay?"

"Okay."

Coach picked up her phone and punched in three numbers. "Isabella? It's Diane." She listened for a moment. "Fine, fine, thanks. Listen, I have a sixth grader here with me." Coach Parks laughed. "Yes, one of my softball players, and she's having a little trouble in Mrs. Hendricks's class." She turned to face Mack and winked. "Uh, not finishing tests on time, spelling, reading."

Mack couldn't believe Coach Parks knew about her reading problems. She bent her head and focused on her shoes. She felt her cheeks get warm and hoped Coach Parks wouldn't notice. The distant sounds of her teammates getting ready for practice made her close her eyes and cringe.

"Thanks, Isabella. I appreciate the favor . . . I know, I know. It shouldn't have to come from me, but . . . Yeah, okay. Thursday during her P.E. class. Perfect. Thanks."

Mack looked up when Coach Parks hung up the phone. She felt like crying, but was too numb for even that.

"That was Mrs. Perez," Coach Parks said. "She's our school psychologist—"

"Psychologist?"

"Yes, she's going to try to help you."

"Why do I have to see a psychologist? Do you think I'm crazy or something?"

Coach Parks laughed. "No, sweetie. Not at all. You're having some trouble with academics, and Mrs. Perez and I just want to help you find out why. I set up an appointment for you on Thursday during P.E. I'll tell Ms. O'Toole that you'll be missing class that day, okay? So don't worry about that."

"Okay." Mack looked at her feet again. "Can I go to practice on Thursday after I see the psychologist?"

"Probably not, kiddo. These things take time. Now, listen, I'll call your Mom this evening and let her know what's going on. Is she waiting for you in the car pool line?"

Mack nodded, but didn't look up. "I called her with Ashley's cell phone."

"Okay, go ahead and take off. We'll figure this out, okay?"

"Okay." Mack snuck out of the P.E. office, praying she wouldn't see any of her teammates. Luckily, she didn't.

On Thursday, Mack knocked on the open door of the school psychologist's office, still not sure why she had to be there.

The dark-skinned woman on the phone put up a finger indicating that she'd be done in a minute.

Mrs. Perez was really pretty. She wore her black hair pulled back into a bun and dressed in a fancy blue business suit. None of Mack's teachers ever wore suits like that. Mrs. Perez kind of looked like J-Lo. Well, an older and darker J-Lo, but still.

Mrs. Perez finished her phone call and looked up. "You must be Mackenzie Kelly."

"Yes, ma'am."

"Please have a seat."

While Mack sat in one of the cushiony red chairs, Mrs. Perez got up and closed the office door. "Well, let's see if we can get you figured out and back on that softball team ASAP. Okay?"

Mack had no idea what "ASAP" meant, but it sounded like Mrs. Perez was on her side.

"Okay, first things first. Study habits. Where do you do your homework?"

"Sometimes at the dining room table, but most times in my room."

"Is the TV or computer on?"

"No. I'm not allowed to watch TV or turn on the computer until my homework's done. I don't have a TV in my room, anyway."

"Do you have a desk in your room?"

"Yes, but I usually sit on my bed."

Mrs. Perez made a note in a folder. "Okay, I'm going to recommend that you use your desk for homework. This will help keep you in the mood."

"Okay." Mack thought that would be impossible. She was rarely in the mood to do homework. Except for math. She could probably do math while running the bases.

"Any brothers and sisters to bother you?"

"No."

"Only child," Mrs. Perez said to the paper as she wrote.

"Okay, now tell me about the troubles you've been having with—" She looked through her file again. "Mrs. Hendricks's English class."

Mack felt her cheeks flush. She wasn't sure she wanted to admit her problems to this stranger, but since Coach Parks seemed to trust her, she would try to do the same.

She unloaded everything. She told Mrs. Perez how mean Mrs. Hendricks was to her and how Halie and the other kids made fun of her. She told Mrs. Perez how she couldn't ever finish those stupid reading tests and how her handwriting was terrible and she couldn't spell. She paused for a while and then told her how dumb she felt all the time.

"Oh, Mackenzie. I'm going to have to disagree with you on that one. Do you know what the Florida Comprehensive Assessment Test is?"

"The FCAT we take every year?"

Mrs. Perez nodded. "I have your FCAT scores in math and science from last year and you are well above grade level in both.

Your file also shows me that you'll be taking Algebra next year as a seventh grader. That's pretty advanced."

Mack smiled.

"Now, here's what I want to do. I want to try and figure out why sixth grader Mackenzie Kelly reads somewhat slower than the rest of the crowd and why she has so much trouble with spelling. In order to do that, I need to test her. Do you think she'll agree to that?"

Mack thought it was kind of funny the way the psychologist acted as if they were talking about another person, but it was kind of fun, too.

"Um, well, Mack doesn't like tests."

Mrs. Perez chuckled. "I'm sure she doesn't, but I'm pretty sure that's where we need to start. The tests aren't for a grade or anything. They're just for my files. What do you say? Can Mack agree to take a two-hour test after school next week?"

"Two hours? She's not going to like that. Do I—oh, I mean, does *she* have to study for it?"

"Absolutely not."

"Oh, thank goodness."

"Why does studying for a test make Mack so anxious?"

Mack spent the rest of the period telling Mrs. Perez all about how school wasn't fun anymore, and since making the softball team, she put up with her classes just so she could play ball after school.

The bell rang and Mrs. Perez stood up. "Come back here on Monday right after school. Okay?"

Mack nodded. "Okay." She couldn't believe how fast the time had gone. She felt like she'd just gotten there. She picked up her backpack and headed to her history class. Maybe seeing the school psychologist wasn't going to be so bad after all, except for the fact that she wasn't allowed to practice with the team.

She'd missed three whole practices that week already, and it didn't look like the end was anywhere in sight. Maybe if she passed that test on Monday she could get back on the team again.

Chapter 13

UCF Golden Knights

Mack sat in the bleachers of the University of Central Florida softball complex with her parents and Ashley. She tried to stay focused on the game, but kept worrying about the big test Mrs. Perez was going to give her after school the next day. If she didn't pass the test she'd probably never get back on her team. She sighed and watched the last Kansas batter ground out to give UCF the win in the first game of the double header.

The UCF softball complex was so big it reminded Mack of *Disney's Wide World of Sports* where the Atlanta Braves had their spring training. Her dad had taken her there for a game the year before.

The UCF outfield was huge, but the outfielders seemed to cover the area pretty easily. The one thing Mack couldn't believe was how fast both the UCF and the Kansas pitchers threw. There was no way she'd ever be able to hit off either one of them. Maybe when she went to college she could, but not now. No way.

All the tickets in the complex were general admission, so when they first got into the stands, she and Ashley had run to the front row bleacher to save four seats right behind home plate. She couldn't believe how close they were to the action. Her dad teased and said they were so close he could smell the home plate umpire's after shave. Mack was more impressed with the free trading cards of the UCF players they got when they first came in. She had carefully placed hers in the back pocket of her shorts.

"So, Stinky," her dad said as the UCF players ran off the field, "how'd you like your first college game?"

Mack couldn't even look at her dad. She was too intent on watching the UCF team high five each other and their coaches.

They had, like, five coaches or something." "I want to play softball in college."

He laughed and said to her mom, "I think she's hooked."

Her mom nodded. "Looks like we might have another UCF Golden Knight in the family."

"Mom." Mack whipped her head around. "I'm going to be a Longhorn at the University of Texas."

"Cow," Ashley teased.

"'Nole," Mack teased back.

Her dad pointed to the UCF gear. "So, why are you wearing your UCF visor and shirt?"

"Father. Mother," she said with mock seriousness. "I am simply supporting your school. It would be rude not to."

"Oh, it's getting kind of thick out here." Her mom waved a hand in front of her nose. She stood up. "Okay, who wants to hit the concession stand?"

Mack's and Ashley's hands shot up.

"Can you get me a hot dog?" her dad asked.

"Sure. C'mon, girls."

They made their way down the bleacher steps and headed toward the concession stand. Mack saw a bunch of kids crowding around some UCF players.

"Mom?"

Her mom turned and saw the UCF players. "Oh, do you girls want to get autographs?"

They nodded vigorously.

She opened her purse and dug out a couple of pens. "Do you have your player cards?"

Mack pulled the cards out of her back pocket.

"Go ahead. I'll get everybody hot dogs. Is that okay?"

Mack nodded, but didn't really care about the hot dogs. She just wanted to meet some real college players.

They tried not to out-and-out run toward the college athletes, but walked with triple speed. They ended up in the back of a loosely-formed line.

Mack looked at the cards in her hand. "Think we'll ever have our picture on cards like these?"

"Heck, yeah, dude. If they have those at Florida State, that is."

"I bet Team USA has cards," Mack suggested with a smile.

"Oh, yeah. They'll probably put a picture of you making a diving catch."

"I don't know how to dive."

"You'll learn because sometimes you have to dive in the outfield. Second base? Not so much."

One of the cards in Mack's hand was a UCF schedule. She couldn't believe how many games they played. She scanned the list, and her eyes almost popped out of her head when she saw that the UCF team was going to play the University of Hawaii. In Hawaii.

"Look, Ash, let's tell my mom and dad we want to go to the UCF game next Saturday and see what they say."

"Awesome, dude. I've never been to Hawaii."

Mack ran her finger down the long list of games, looking for other exotic places the team might travel to. She ran through the games in February, and her finger hit the name of a certain well-known team. She forgot to breathe.

"Ashley."

"What?"

"Read that name for me. I think I'm hallucinating."

"Where?" She looked where Mack pointed. "Holy wow. You're kidding."

"It says it, doesn't it?"

"Yeah."

"Cat Osterman's coming," Mack gushed. "I'm actually gonna see her."

"I can't believe UCF is playing Team USA. When?" She looked at the schedule again. "At the end of February."

"It must be their get-ready-for-the-Olympics tour or something."

"Yeah."

"Eeeee," they squealed and hugged each other.

Mack couldn't believe how jiggly her stomach felt when she thought about seeing Cat Osterman and Jessica Mendoza and

Natasha Watley and Jennie Finch and Lisa Fernandez and Lovieanne Jung and Laura Berg, and, ahh, just seeing all of them in person.

But then reality hit, and she remembered that she wasn't on the school team anymore. A black ache spread from somewhere deep inside her chest, kind of like when Grandma Kelly died. So she did the only thing she knew how to do—she tried to ignore it and held onto the idea that Mrs. Perez's two-hour test on Monday would get her reinstated on the team ASAP. She'd found out from her mom that ASAP meant "as soon as possible."

"Stop," Ashley said.

"What?"

"Stop thinking. I can see it on your face, dude. Everything's going to work out. Taylor hates playing center field and everybody misses you. So, don't worry about it. You'll do great on your test on Monday and show them that it's all Mrs. Hendricks's fault."

"I'm trying to stay positive, but it's hard."

They finally made it to the front of the line, and she fanned out her cards to the tall player standing in front of her. The player laughed and pulled out the card with her picture on it. She signed her name and handed it back to Mack. Mack looked down at the card and realized that standing right in front of her was Ashley Van Ryn, the UCF center fielder. While watching the game against Kansas, she imagined she was Van Ryn in center field, backing up the infielders and chasing down ground balls.

Mack swallowed hard, but couldn't think of anything to say to Van Ryn except, "Thanks." She said it in such a shy and timid voice that she surprised herself. The UCF center fielder smiled again and reached for Ashley's card.

Down the line they went until they were face to face with number ten, Allison Kime—the UCF pitcher who pitched a thousand miles an hour. Mack stood there with her mouth hanging open while the pretty blonde signed her card.

Allison smiled at her, and Mack remembered her manners. "Thank you."

She had never been this close to sports' superstars before. What was she going to do when she actually saw Cat Osterman? She'd probably faint or something.

Ashley nudged her out of the way, and Mack felt the all-too-familiar sting of tears in her eyes. The college game she had just seen made her feel a little, no a lot, lost. She just had to get back on her own team ASAP because she desperately wanted to play softball at Winterford High School and then at the University of Texas and then for Team USA and then maybe even for a professional team like the Rockford Thunder where Cat Osterman played. She wanted those things more than anything, more than a cell phone and more than a passing grade in Mrs. Hendricks's class. But evil Mrs. Hendricks and the evil IOC were scheming to take all of that away from her before she had a chance to get started.

Mack took a deep breath and stabbed at the tears in her eyes. She didn't want Ashley to see her crying.

"Dude, I got Allison Keem's autograph."

"Me, too, but it's pronounced Kime. Like lime."

"Oh, sorry. You okay, dude?"

Mack took a deep breath and looked away as tears welled up again. "No, I'm not."

Chapter 14

Results

Mack sat in Mrs. Perez's office waiting for her mom to come from the main office. She silently counted the number of days until Team USA came to Florida to play UCF—fifteen. She counted the number of practices she'd missed with her team so far—eight. She counted the number of days before the team's first game—two. Or three if today counted. And she counted the number of players whose names she could remember from the UCF softball team—six. She was just about to start counting the number of Team USA players when her mom knocked lightly on Mrs. Perez's open door.

"Hi, Mom." Mack stood up and gave her a hug. "Happy Valentine's Day."

"Happy Valentine's Day to you, too, honey." She shook hands with Mrs. Perez. "I hope I'm not late."

"Not at all. I'm glad we finally got a chance to meet after so many phone conversations." Mrs. Perez laughed. "Go ahead and have a seat. I have Mack's test results right here."

"Did I pass?" Mack craned her neck to see the results.

"Mack," Mrs. Perez admonished, "I told you it wasn't that kind of test. You took a diagnostic test so we can figure out how you tick."

"Oh." She must have failed.

"Well, I've figured out why Mack's been having so much trouble. It's what I suspected, actually."

"Okay." The nervous tone in her mom's voice made Mack nervous, too.

"Mack has a learning disability. I prefer to call it a learning *difference* instead of a disability."

I have a disability? I need a wheelchair? Mack swung her legs back and forth to test them. *I feel fine.*

"And I believe that this young lady has already developed some amazing compensatory strategies," Mrs. Perez continued.

"She has a learning disability?" her mom repeated. "What exactly does that mean?"

"Well, I don't want to scare you with a label, but Mack has dyslexia."

"Oh." The surprise in her mom's voice scared Mack a little.

"What's that mean?" Mack asked.

"Well, it means that reading for you is probably exhausting," Mrs. Perez answered. "It's hard for you to sound out words, and you most likely mix up similar words—like *now* and *know*. Because you're spending so much energy trying to figure out each and every word, the larger meaning gets lost."

"Yeah," Mack said with relief. Somebody finally understood. "It's like once I get to the end of a paragraph, I forgot what the first part said."

Her mom nodded. "So, what do we do now?"

"Well, first of all, Mrs. Kelly, please understand that this isn't your or your husband's fault. In fact, five percent of kids her age have processing issues like dyslexia. Mack and I will work together to come up with strategies to help her. I want you to remember that she is *not* mentally deficient. She just processes things differently. Here's an analogy I think Mack will understand. You like softball, right?"

"Yes, ma'am."

"Most people throw overhand, right? Like this?" Mrs. Perez mimicked throwing a ball overhand which was kind of weird because she had long red fingernails and wore a fancy business suit. "But then there are a few who throw sidearm." She mimicked throwing sidearm.

"Yeah, Marci sometimes throws sidearm and Coach yells at her."

Mrs. Perez laughed. "Well, your friend Marci has a throwing difference, but she can still throw the ball, right?"

"Oh, like I have a learning difference, but I can still learn."

"Exactly. I'd like us to work together three days a week so I can help you master different learning tools."

Mack sat up taller. "And put them in my repertoire."

Her mom laughed. "Where did you learn such a word?"

"Coach Parks."

Mrs. Perez chuckled. "Yes, I suppose that's a good way to describe it. We'll come up with learning strategies for your learning repertoire. The first thing we'll implement is extended time on tests."

"Mrs. Hendricks never lets me have more time. Ever."

"Well, Mrs. Hendricks is going to have to allow you extra time."

"Why?"

"Because it's the law."

"The law?" her mom asked.

"Yes, the Individuals with Disabilities Education Act—again I'm not a fan of the word disability—but the Act ensures that everyone who needs special services gets it. So Mack and I will come up with her IEP—Individual Education Plan—which will most definitely include extended time testing."

"It's the law, Mom."

"And, actually," Mrs. Perez added, "we have Mrs. Hendricks to thank."

"Why?" Mack said way too quickly. She didn't mean to be rude.

"Because without her pulling you off the softball team, Coach Parks never would have called me to help you."

"Can I practice today?"

"Not yet. I'm sorry. Let's start meeting on a regular basis next week. We'll meet during your P.E. period on Mondays, Wednesdays, and Thursdays. Okay?" Without waiting for Mack to answer, Mrs. Perez turned to her mom. "I have some good strategies I think will work here. She's a very bright girl."

They stood up to leave, and Mack asked her mom the question that had been kind of bugging her ever since Mrs. Perez had first used the word disability. "Mom, am I retarded?"

"No, honey. I guess you just learn differently than other people."

"Mack, have you heard of Tom Cruise?" Mrs. Perez leaned in the doorway of her office.

"Yes, ma'am."

"He has dyslexia."

"No way."

Mrs. Perez nodded. "And lots of other people have had learning issues like you. People like Magic Johnson, Albert Einstein, Thomas Edison, and Alexander Graham Bell."

"Those are all guys."

"Okay, how about Cher or Whoopi Goldberg or Keira Knightley."

"Keira Knightly from the pirate movies?"

"Yes, and all those people are pretty successful, aren't they?"

Mack nodded.

"It was nice meeting you, Mrs. Kelly. And I'll see you next week, Mack."

Mack walked with her mom toward the main office. She wondered what having dyslexia really meant. Mrs. Perez's test firmly proved without a doubt that she was different than everybody else.

She sighed. She didn't want to be different. What would Ashley think? Worse yet, what would Halie and her Chipettes think?

Her mom signed out at the front desk and gave Mack an overlong hug. She squeezed a little tighter than usual, and Mack knew that she was trying to tell her that everything would turn out all right.

Mack wasn't so sure, but to lighten the mood she asked, "What did Alexander Graham Bell invent?"

"The telephone. You know that."

"Can I get one?" She grinned.

"Oh, you are relentless, child."

Chapter 15

Praying for Rain

Even though Mack prayed and prayed for rain, puffy white clouds drifted overhead in the crystal blue sky. Her parents had left the decision about going to the game completely up to her, and so there they sat on Saturday morning waiting for the Glenda Hood Middle School Hawks to play the Orangeville Owls in the first softball game of the season.

"Can you smell the umpire's perfume, Dad?"

Her dad laughed. "Yeah, we've got nice seats here." He tapped the metal bleacher twice.

"I know a better seat."

"Oh, yeah? Where?"

She pointed to the dugout.

Her dad tried to hold back a sigh, but Mack heard it. "Well, you and Mrs. Perez are going to fix that sidearm of yours soon, right?"

"My sidearm?" Mack was confused for a second, but then she remembered telling him about Mrs. Perez's softball story. "Oh, yeah, my *sidearm*. But, how long 'til I can play again?"

"These things take time," her mom said quietly, "but Mrs. Perez said she'll be in touch with us every week."

"Every week? Like more than one?"

Her mom nodded and shrugged.

Mack looked to the sky, hoping to see a big fat rain cloud moving in. No such luck. Her stomach clenched when her team ran onto the field to start the game. She didn't know what to do with herself, because she wanted so badly to be the one running out to center field. To occupy herself, she took off her Team USA visor and redid her ponytail with a twist of her orange scrunchie. She chose orange because orange and black were the Hood Middle

School colors. Even though she wasn't on the team anymore she wanted to support Ashley and Taylor and Kristina and Marci and, oh, just the whole team, including Coach Parks who went to bat for her with Mrs. Hendricks. And maybe even Halie. Maybe.

"Go, Ashley," Mack called out to her friend at second base.

Ashley smiled, but couldn't wave or anything because she was a little busy. This was the first game after all.

Mack sat with pins and needles, watching Kristina pitch the first inning. She cheered loudly as three Owls batters got up and promptly got out, one-two-three.

Ashley stepped up to the plate as the first batter for the Hawks and that familiar black feeling returned.

"Go Ash. C'mon Hawks," Mack yelled. Even though Ashley was her best friend, it kind of hurt to watch her lead off, because Coach Parks told Mack she was going to be the lead off batter.

Mack noticed the first baseman hanging way back past the bag. *Drop down a bunt, Ash,* Mack thought, but Ashley apparently couldn't read minds, because she slapped the ball right to the first baseman and was out before she even made it a quarter of the way up the line.

The Owls' pitcher was fairly consistent and the first three Hawks batters got out right away, keeping the game scoreless after the first inning. The score was still zip to zip when the Hawks came up to hit in the bottom of the sixth inning.

Ashley walked to lead off the inning followed quickly by a single to left field by Marci. With runners on first and second, Taylor got up to bat and smacked a single up the middle to score Ashley from second base. That was the only run the Hawks would get that inning, but at least they were ahead one to nothing. All they had to do was make sure the Owls didn't score any runs in the top of the seventh inning and they would win.

Stephanie, the Hawks' catcher, made the last out of the inning and needed time to get her catcher's gear back on, so Halie threw on the catcher's mask, pulled her blonde ponytail out from behind the straps, and squatted low behind the plate.

Kristina threw two pitches to her, and Mack was surprised when Halie successfully scooped up the second pitch that was in the dirt. By this time, Stephanie was ready so Halie popped back up and whisked the mask off her head.

Halie passed Mack on her way to the dugout. She narrowed her eyes and glared. "Where's your uniform, Mack? Couldn't you read the name on the shirt?"

A bunch of Halie's Chipettes burst out laughing in the dugout. Mack looked away, embarrassed that her parents heard.

"That little brat," her mom muttered under her breath, her cheeks turned bright red.

"Mom, don't listen to her. She doesn't bother me." It wasn't exactly the truth, but she didn't want her mom to worry. "Okay?"

"Okay, honey." Her mom patted her on the shoulder.

The Owls hit into two quick outs, so the Hawks had only one out to go before they won their first game. The crowd groaned when Kristina walked the next batter in four pitches.

The shortstop from the Owls' team stepped into the batter's box and dug in with her cleats. She took a mighty practice swing and readied herself for the pitch. Kristina threw a fast ball, and the Owls' shortstop slammed the pitch into the seven-eight gap between left and center fields.

Mack leaped up and cringed as Taylor ran at the wrong angle, allowing the ball to skip all the way to the fence. After what seemed like an hour, Taylor reached the ball, but by that time the runner on first had scored and the batter was on her way to third base. The crowd, including Mack, groaned as the ball squirted out of Taylor's hand at the fence. Taylor tried again and heaved the ball to Beth at shortstop.

"Home. Home," Mack yelled with the rest of the people in the stands.

The Owls' base runner rounded third and was almost home when Beth relayed the ball. The ball reached Stephanie at home plate just as the runner slid. Mack groaned when the home plate umpire threw her arms out to both sides and yelled, "Safe."

The Hawks' fans loudly protested the call. They clearly had a different opinion than the umpire, but, honestly, it looked like the Owls' shortstop had beaten the throw and slid in safely.

The Hawks weren't able to score in the bottom half of the seventh inning and they lost their first game by a score of 1-2. Mack stood up and blew out a sigh, knowing she could have helped her team. She might have been able to get to the ball at the fence a lot faster than Taylor, or she might have even been able to catch the monster fly ball in the first place. There was nothing she could do about it, though, because she wasn't on the team. She was just a spectator.

The black ache in her chest started up again. Stupid dyslexia didn't stop Keira Knightley from making movies and stupid dyslexia wasn't going to keep her from playing ball, either. She was going to pass the next stupid English test and she was going to get back on the team. In the meantime, all she had to do was keep praying for rain.

Chapter 16

Lemonade

The Golden Knights ran off the field after the top of the second inning. Mack squirmed on the hard bleachers. She wanted to feel happy about watching her favorite UCF players, but instead, felt anxious. She had been working with Mrs. Perez for a whole week now, but she still didn't know when she could rejoin the team. She was beginning to think she'd never be able to play again, especially if Mrs. Hendricks had anything to do with it. She tried not to show that she was bummed out because Ashley was sitting right next to her on the bleachers and her parents were sitting right behind.

"Where the heck is the Drake team from, anyway?" Ashley asked.

Mack shrugged and adjusted her UCF visor.

"Des Moines, Iowa," her mom said.

"Iowa?" Ashley said. "That's pretty far away, isn't it?"

"Yeah." Mack pointed at her program. "There's a team from Michigan here, too."

"This is spring training for those teams," her dad said. "It's probably still snowing where they're from."

"Dad, it's almost March."

"It stays cold in the north for a long time. Sometimes it snows in April."

Mack and Ashley exchanged a look of disbelief.

"No way am I going to college in the north," Mack said.

"Me, either."

The first UCF batter of the inning got up, and Mack remembered what Mrs. Perez said in their very first session. "When life gives you lemons, make lemonade." Mack wasn't exactly sure what she meant at the time, but her mom explained that it meant she should try to make the best of things in a bad situation. So even though her life had been shaken up pretty badly recently, she tried to focus on the good things.

With that in mind, Mack had put in a lot of seat time at her desk in her room. She stopped watching TV, except for anything softball related, of course, and she spent at least an hour more on her homework than usual. Mrs. Perez's new study strategies weren't really that hard, just time-consuming. Like the list of unfamiliar words she had to make while reading. She had to write down any strange word, define it, and then ask her mom or dad how to pronounce it. The many tricks and strategies that Mrs. Perez gave her to try were almost too much, but if they got her back on the team, then she would try them all.

She had already missed three whole weeks of practice and two whole games, so when she wasn't working on school stuff she practiced softball with her dad. He even treated the lawn for those stupid fire ants so they wouldn't get bitten up when they played catch after dinner every night in the backyard. They even went to the batting cages in Longwood where she hit about a hundred balls each time. A couple of times, she and her dad went down to the elementary school so he could hit her fly balls. Of course, she ended every session running the bases five times in a row.

Mack clapped and shouted, "Go UCF!" as the first UCF batter walked in the bottom of the second inning.

"Dude," Ashley said, "I'm thinking sacrifice bunt right about now. What do you think?"

"Absolutely, with no outs, they have to move the runner over."

The UCF batter squared to bunt, and Mack and Ashley punched fists.

"Dude, we should be coaches."

"Absolutely."

"You should ask Coach Parks if you can sit in the dugout with us during games."

"I'm not sure. I'm kind of not on the team."

"But you're gonna be back on the team any day now, right?" Ashley grinned.

"I'm not so sure about that because Mrs. Hendricks is so—" Mack wanted to say "evil" but remembered that her parents were sitting right behind her. "So hard to please."

"How was your test on Friday?"

"Ooh." Mack yelled in sympathy as the next UCF batter got hit by a pitch to put runners on first and second. "I thought I did really good. With that extra time, I could finally breathe during a test."

"See? Now Mrs. Hendricks will know that you can do it and she'll have to let you back on the team."

"Maybe." Mack didn't think it would be that easy. "Go Ashley," she yelled to her center field counterpart, Ashley Van Ryn, who had just stepped into the batter's box.

Mack cheered when both base runners advanced on a wild pitch. She cheered even louder when the Drake shortstop made an error, and Van Ryn reached first base safely. That put UCF up by a score of 1-0. Mack and Ashley cheered wildly when Van Ryn then stole second base to put runners on second and third with one out.

"That's going to be you soon," Ashley said. "The center fielder who steals bases."

They clapped when the next batter walked to load the bases, but then groaned when the batter after that struck out for the second out of the inning.

"I can't believe I struck out twice against Tuskford on Tuesday," Ashley said.

"That's because you let the pitcher get in your head."

"What do you mean?"

"Tuskford has to be the worst team in the league, but everybody heard about the new pitcher they got from California, and you all got scared."

"Yeah, but she was really good," Ashley said almost under her breath.

"Yeah, but our Kristina's better."

"You think so?"

"Absolutely."

"Too bad our game was rained out yesterday," Ashley said. "I wanted to play."

"I know the feeling, but actually . . ."

"What?"

"I prayed for the rain."

"What?" Ashley slapped Mack playfully in the arm. "Why?"

"Because I don't want to get too far behind."

"Oh, that's cool, dude. I probably would have done the same thing."

Mack and Ashley stood up and stomped their feet when an error by the Drake third baseman allowed another UCF runner to score.

"Two nothing, dude."

"Whoo-hoo." Mack was positively giddy.

As it turned out, those were the only runs the UCF team would get but they were enough to win the game 2-1.

"So do you girls want to play at UCF for Coach Leurs-Gillespie?" her dad asked as they stood up to leave the stadium.

Mack didn't want to admit it, but she kind of liked the idea. A lot. But didn't say so. "Didn't they say she has, like, almost five hundred wins or something?"

"Almost. She's getting close. Maybe we'll be in the stands when it happens," her dad said.

Mack smiled. "That'd be awesome."

"Do you girls want to go to Pollo Tropical for lunch?" her mom asked.

"Yeah," they said together.

"Hot salsa bar. Woo hoo," Ashley said.

"Our treat, Ashley."

"Thanks, Mrs. Kelly."

They headed toward the parking lot.

"And how about the batting cages after that?" Mack's dad suggested with a grin.

"Thanks, Dad."

"Yeah, thanks, Mr. Kelly. I could use some batting practice," Ashley said. "We haven't won a single game yet."

Mack's all-too-familiar sick feeling crept into her stomach. She might not be playing for *any* college team if she didn't get back on the team soon. She tried to stay positive like Mrs. Perez wanted her too, but there wasn't enough lemonade in the world to make her feel better at that moment.

Chapter 17

Reaching Your Potential

"Mackenzie, would you come up here, please?" Mrs. Hendricks stood behind her desk, peering down at Mack over her glasses.

"Yes, ma'am." Mack got up slowly. It was time for her Monday walk of shame. Once again, everyone else got their Friday test back except for her.

She stood in front of the desk with her head down, waiting to be slaughtered.

"How many sessions have you had with Mrs. Perez?"

"Three."

"Just three?"

"Yes, ma'am."

"Well, Mrs. Perez is a miracle worker, because . . ." Mrs. Hendricks placed Mack's test face up on her desk with the grade showing.

Mack couldn't believe what she saw. "I got a B? Me? I got a B?"

Mrs. Hendricks nodded. "I think the extended time really helped you. The other kids griped about you getting more time, but if you can pull out a B, then I'm all for it."

Mack's heart was pounding. She had never, ever, gotten a B on anything in Mrs. Hendricks's class. This was like hitting a walk off home run to win a game. "I can't believe it."

"Well, believe it. Your test wasn't perfect by any means, but you showed a vast improvement."

"Thanks." Mack blew out a sigh in relief.

Mack started to turn to go back to her seat.

Mrs. Hendricks cleared her throat. "So, tell me, Mackenzie. What exactly have you and Mrs. Perez been working on?"

"Well, um. She taught me a lot of things. Like to use two rulers on the page when I read so I can focus on just one line at a time. That's kind of cool. She told me to read out loud so I hear the words. My mom and dad and Mrs. Perez help me with the pronunciation sometimes. Mrs. Perez says that when I read out loud I use a different modality to strengthen neural connections, but I have no idea what that means."

Mrs. Hendricks laughed. "Well, whatever it means, it seems to be working."

"And the weird part is that when they help me pronounce the words, I already know some of them. I just didn't put together what they looked like on paper and how they sounded. A lot of words make more sense now. Oh, and," Mack continued excitedly, "my dad is going to find some books on tape. That'll help me understand all those stories we read."

"Yes, as a matter of fact, I emailed your father the reading list this morning."

"Cool. Thanks." Mack was so excited she had trouble keeping still. "Oh, and now I write down all the vocabulary words that I don't know and use a dictionary to look them up. All that takes a lot of time, though."

Mrs. Hendricks nodded. "I'm sure it does. Now that you're finally putting in some effort, you're making good progress. In fact, when your teachers met with Mrs. Perez last week—"

"My teachers met? To talk about me?" Mack had no idea stuff like that happened at Hood Middle School.

"Yes, Mrs. Perez had a meeting to discuss your IEP. Do you know what that is?"

"Um, my Individual Education something."

"Individual Education *Plan*. At the meeting, your teachers, including me, kept saying how bright you were and how you just weren't quite reaching your potential. I'm glad we found a way to help you. Having said that, I'm also pleased to let you know that you've been reinstated on your baseball team."

Mack barely heard the last thing because she was focusing on the fact that her teachers said she was bright. If Mrs. Hendricks thought she was smart, then why hadn't she ever shared that before? All this time, she thought she was dumb.

Mrs. Hendricks cleared her throat. "That means you can rejoin your team."

Mack finally registered the words. "Really? No way." She hoped beyond hope that Mrs. Hendricks wasn't just playing a mean trick on her.

"Well, to be honest, I still think it's too soon, but Mrs. Perez and the other teachers thought it was a good idea to let you participate on your baseball team. I just hope you can handle all of this, Mackenzie." Mrs. Hendricks peered at Mack over the top of her reading glasses with a doubtful look.

"Yes, ma'am," Mack said. Mrs. Hendricks sure had a way of making awesome news sound bad.

"Coach Parks will be expecting you at practice this very afternoon." Mrs. Hendricks put up a cautionary finger. "However, young lady, your continuance on this baseball team of yours is directly related to your grades in this class. So I expect you to work hard on your new strategies and continue to get your grades up."

"Yes, ma'am." The frenzied joy she had held in check came bursting back up as soon as she turned away. She had to tell Ashley. She didn't have practice clothes. She didn't have her glove. She didn't have her bat. She had to call her mom. These and a thousand other thoughts raced through her head. She walked back to her seat completely ignoring Halie.

Chapter 18

She's Got It

Coach Parks substituted Mack into the game in the bottom of the fourth inning. Mack grabbed her Jessica Mendoza bat and knew she looked scared to death. She tried to keep her hands from shaking as she put her batting helmet on her head. To top things off, the Hood Hawks were playing the Redlake Pirates, a team that always gave them trouble.

Thank goodness the game with the Pinegrove Lions had been rained out on Saturday, otherwise the Hawks might be 0-3, instead of just 0-2. At least they weren't losing against the Pirates because the score was tied up 3-3 in the bottom of the fourth.

Mack dug her cleats into the lefty box and took a practice swing. The Pirates' pitcher supposedly had a lot of different pitches—a fast ball, a change-up, a curve ball, and a drop ball. Kristina and Halie were working on their drops, but she hadn't yet seen a really effective drop ball.

Mack swallowed hard and readied herself for the pitch. The ball looked like it was coming in for a strike, but then suddenly fell and hit the dirt. The catcher blocked the ball with her mitt. Mack knew instantly she had just witnessed a drop ball.

She had missed something like fifteen practices while she was off the team, but felt like she'd missed the entire season. Her knees started to shake, so she put her left hand up. "Time, please."

"Time." The umpire stood up and put both hands in the air.

Mack stepped out of the box and took a deep breath. Mrs. Perez told her she could do anything if she put her mind to it. She hoped that worked in softball, too.

She stepped back in the batter's box and the Pirate's pitcher delivered the pitch. Mack slid her front foot back and stepped forward with her left. The pitch was just about there and she could tell it wasn't going to drop. She tapped a bunt onto the infield and ran as fast as she could to first base.

"Safe," the umpire in the field yelled.

Mack couldn't believe it. In her first at-bat in her first game on her first school team, she got on base. She smiled when the Hawks' fans cheered for her. She readied herself to run the bases while Ashley stepped into the batter's box. Mack watched Coach Parks for the signs. Shoulder. S for steal. She was ready.

The pitcher released the ball, and Mack took off for second base. She slid in safely. The throw from the catcher wasn't even close. On the next pitch, Ashley slapped the ball, but ended up grounding out. Luckily Mack was able to get to third on the play. Marci was up next and tried to bunt for a hit, but was thrown out at first for the second out of the inning.

Mack wanted desperately to score the go-ahead run to prove to everybody that even though she had missed three weeks, she still deserved to be on the team.

Taylor, up next, dug her heels in the box. She wound up and swung hard. The ball skipped right past Mack on third base and into left field.

Mack pumped her fists and sprinted home for the go-ahead run. The next batter struck out, so after the end of four innings, the Hawks were beating the troublesome Pirates by a score of 4-3.

The score remained unchanged through the fifth and sixth innings, and at the top of the seventh inning, Mack grabbed her Cat Osterman glove and ran out to center field. If they could hold them, then the run that Mack scored in the fourth would be the game-winner.

"I am sooooo glad you're back, Rookie," Taylor called from left field and threw her a warm-up ball. "I hate playing center field."

"That's what I heard." Mack threw the ball back. "I'm glad I'm back, too."

"Coming down," Stephanie yelled from behind the plate, and Ashley ran to second base for the throw. That was the cue for the outfielders to put their gloves together in center field. Mack had seen the UCF team do that, and Coach Parks thought it was an excellent idea.

"On three," Taylor said. "One, two, three."

"Stick together."

Taylor and Marci ran back to their respective positions while Mack pounded her glove. She was ready for whatever the Redlake Pirates sent her way.

The first Pirate batter of the inning struck out. The second Pirate batter conveniently grounded out to Ashley at second base. Mack backed her up and high-fived her before heading back out to center. Coach Parks motioned for the outfielders to take a couple of steps back when the big Pirates' first baseman stepped up to bat.

The Pirates' first baseman swung at the first pitch and blasted a ball deep down the left field line. Foul. Taylor ran after the ball and tossed it back in. She motioned for Mack to take a few steps toward her and a few steps back. The next two swings were also cannon shots down the left field line, foul again. Mack figured that if this batter ever got the ball fair it would be Taylor's for sure.

Stephanie moved her catcher's mitt to the outside of the plate which meant that the ball might get hit to center. Before Mack could fully form the thought, the ball sailed in her direction.

"Rookie," Taylor shouted. "School, school, school. Back. Back."

Mack pumped her arms and took off toward the fence in the direction of the school. She leaped into the air and hoped she'd timed it right. The ball thwacked inside her glove. She closed it quickly, but the momentum from her leap pushed her over. She tucked her shoulder underneath and rolled the way she'd learned to do in P.E.

After rolling completely over, she sat on the ground, trying to get the world to right itself. The umpire came running up on her, and Mack wasn't sure what she was supposed to do, so she held up her glove with the ball in it.

"She's got it. The batter's out," the umpire yelled and threw an arm in the air.

The cheering from the crowd made Mack's insides jittery. Taylor and Marci ran over to help her get up.

"Awesome dive, Rookie." Taylor hugged her. *It wasn't really a dive,* Mack thought. *It was more of a leap and then a roll so I wouldn't break my face.* "That was amazing," Marci said. "We're so glad you're back." Mack smiled so big it almost split her face. The Hawks had just won their first game by a score of 4-3. She ran back to her team's dugout, thinking that maybe diving wasn't so hard after all. If she wanted to play outfield like Jessica Mendoza, she had to add diving to her softball repertoire ASAP. Thinking about Jessica Mendoza made her remember that Team USA would be there in only four more days. Her stomach went into double, no triple, jiggles.

Chapter 19

Cat Comes to Town

Everybody in Central Florida, it seemed, had heard about Team USA coming to play UCF. Mack and Ashley squeezed up against the fence elbow to elbow with the other fans, hoping to get a closer look at the Team USA players.

"There she is." Ashley pointed.

"Where?" As soon as Mack asked the question, she saw tall number eight in the dugout. "I see her." She knew she was starstruck, but she couldn't help it. Cat Osterman was standing one softball infield away from her. "I wish we were on the other side."

"I know. Holy wow, here they come."

Mack adjusted her University of Texas visor, hoping that Cat would see it. She and Ashley held out their hands as the members of the Olympic team ran along the fence high-fiving the fans. She practically fainted when Cat Osterman slapped her five, pointed to the Texas visor, and smiled as she ran on.

Mack finally remembered to breathe and realized that Cat was really tall. All the Team USA pitchers were tall, including Jennie Finch who was going to be the starting pitcher that night. Mack was disappointed that Cat wasn't pitching, but at least she had just high-fived her hero.

"C'mon." Ashley pulled on her arm. "Let's go back to our seats. My dad said they'll probably do autographs after the game."

Reluctantly, Mack agreed and let Ashley lead the way to their dads in the bleachers. She liked Mr. Ames, Ashley's dad. He had big broad shoulders and thinning light brown hair, which he usually kept covered with an FSU baseball hat. His mustache, on the other hand, was thick and full. Her own dad didn't have one because he said it felt like a fuzzy caterpillar sleeping under his nose.

Before they left the house, Mack asked her mom if she was coming to the game, but her mom said, "No, I'm going to stay home, take a long hot bath, and read a book." It sounded kind of boring to Mack. How could you stay home when Cat Osterman was in town?

"So, are you ever going to wash that hand again?" her dad asked when she sat on the bleachers.

Mack laughed and looked down at her right hand. "Probably not."

She almost felt like she was dreaming as she watched Team USA take the field. Jessica Mendoza ran to left field, and Caitlin Lowe ran to center. She smiled wider when she saw Laura Berg in right field. Her dad had told her that Laura Berg's nickname was "Grandma" because she had been on the team so long. She didn't think Berg looked like a Grandma at all and she wanted to be just like her and win three gold medals or more. 2008 would make four if they won. No—*when* they won. She crossed her fingers, hoping she hadn't just jinxed the team.

The first three UCF batters struck out one-two-three.

Mack drew a quick breath between her clenched teeth. "It's not looking good for the Golden Knights."

"I know, but they're not supposed to win, anyway."

"That's true. Oh, look. There's Ashley Van Ryn running out to center field."

"And there's Allison Kime. Of course she's pitching, but Team USA'll probably hit like three hundred home runs off her, dude." Ashley shook her head as if dreading the beating UCF was about to take at the hands of the Olympic team.

"Yeah, and Crystl Bustos will probably hit sixty homers by herself, but, I hope not. I want UCF to make it a close game."

"Keep dreamin', dude. Keep dreamin'."

Kime struck out both Natasha Watley and Jessica Mendoza causing Team USA to go down one-two-three in the bottom of the first inning.

Mack nudged Ashley with her shoulder. "So much for three hundred home runs."

"Yeah. I can't believe it."

The UCF team came up to bat in the top of the second inning, and Mack couldn't help overhearing her dad's conversation with Ashley's dad.

"I heard some of the IOC members have never even seen a softball game," her dad said, "and they still voted it out of the next Olympics."

"Well," Ashley's dad said, "the United States dominated the last three Olympics. In 2004 they had eight shutouts and outscored everybody else fifty or fifty-one to one. Something like that. The IOC might not think too highly about that."

"Who got the only run?" her dad wondered out loud.

"I know," Mack said.

"Oh, yeah? Who?"

"I'll tell you if I can have a cell phone."

"A cell phone? At this rate, you'll be lucky if you get a phone by the time you go to college."

Mack stuck out her lower lip, but she knew her dad was kidding. "Okay, fine. Australia scored the only run."

"How'd you know that, Stinky?"

"Taylor told us. Right, Ash?"

"Yeah," Ashley agreed. "Australia scored once in the gold medal game in Athens in 2004."

"Our girls are so smart," Ashley's dad said. "The United States won gold in Atlanta, then Sydney, and then Athens. I mean, if they win gold again in Beijing this summer, we may never get softball back."

Mack thought that was the worst thing she'd ever heard. The IOC shouldn't punish the United States for playing well. That would be like studying really hard for a test, getting an A-plus, and then getting in trouble for it. That made no sense at all.

"Well," her dad said, "maybe the rest of the world will catch up to us by 2012, but maybe that's not it. Maybe softball got tied in with baseball. We don't send our pros to the Olympics and major league baseball has a huge steroids problem, too. Maybe the IOC felt spiteful about that."

"Who knows? I just hope they come to their senses, soon."

"Me, too," Mack butted back in.

Team USA swapped out pitchers in the top of the third inning, but Mack was disappointed when Lisa Fernandez went in to pitch instead of Cat. She liked Lisa Fernandez, too, so it was kind of cool to watch her pitch, but it was still kind of weird watching Cat in the dugout cheering on her teammates.

"Dude, maybe she'll go in later," Ashley said.

But later never came, because in the top of the sixth inning Monica Abbott went in to pitch for Team USA.

"Team USA's used three pitchers already, but UCF still has Kime in," Mack said.

"Why take her out?" her dad asked. "She's got a one-hitter going."

"Just one hit?" Mack asked. "Oh, yeah. Tairia Flowers hit that double."

Ashley pointed to the UCF dugout. "I can't believe nobody has scored yet."

Mack grinned. "Our little University of Central Florida is hanging with the big dogs."

Her dad smiled at her with an all-knowing expression.

"Oh, c'mon," Mack said. "You didn't know UCF was this good, either."

UCF didn't produce a base runner in the top of the sixth inning, and Mack started getting antsy. "Dad, it's still zero to zero. How come Team USA hasn't even scored?"

"I don't know. Maybe they're tired. They're on a tour of the entire country playing all kinds of colleges and all-star teams."

"Yeah, but they should have scored at least one run by now."

In the bottom of the sixth inning, Natasha Watley led off the inning. Mack waited for her to slap or bunt for a hit. Instead, Kime struck her out.

Her dad must have sensed her disappointment. "Happens to the best of us."

Mack's spirits rose when one of her other idols, Jessica Mendoza, laid down a bunt for a hit and got on base. She didn't stay there long because she promptly stole second on the UCF catcher Lindsay Dean.

"Looks like you, dude," Ashley said, pointing at Mendoza on second.

"I wish."

Crystl Bustos struck out to make two outs in the top of the sixth, and it looked as if the game might remain scoreless going into the seventh inning. Andrea Duran, Team USA's third baseman, got up to bat. Her single to right field brought Mendoza in to score.

"Now she really looks like you, dude."

"Someday that's going to be you and me out there."

Ashley nodded, and they punched fists.

Mack was glad Team USA finally scored, but kind of felt bad, too, when UCF didn't answer the run in the top of the seventh inning and lost the game 1-0.

"Can we get autographs, Dad?" Mack held out her pen and the Team USA cards they had gotten when they walked into the complex.

"How could I stop you? Go on. Mr. Ames and I'll wait for you right here."

Mack ran over to the crowd forming around Cat Osterman and tried to remember to breathe.

Chapter 20

Go Jump!

Mack took a deep breath, trying to calm down before the game started that Saturday morning, but every time she thought about seeing the Olympic team play UCF the night before, she got all oogly inside. As soon as she'd gotten home, she carefully framed her Cat Osterman autograph and displayed it proudly on her desk.

Mack sprinted out to center field at the start of the game and wasn't sure her feet actually touched the ground. Coach Parks let her start the game in center instead of substituting her in later, and this was only her second game since coming back.

"Hey, Rook," Taylor called. "Ready to kick some Seagull butt?"

"Yeah, then we won't have a losing record." The last thing Mack wanted to do was lose the game and end up with a horrible 1-3 record. She pounded her glove and waited for Halie to throw the first pitch.

Halie walked the first batter of the game and Mack groaned. Halie walked the second batter and Mack mumbled, "C'mon, Halie. Get your act together." Halie then walked the third batter on four pitches to load the bases. Mack took a deep breath and yelled, "C'mon, Hawks. No outs, any base. We can do this."

According to Taylor, the Jamestown Seagulls were their archrivals and beating them meant more than just a tally in their win column. It meant bragging rights, too, since the two middle schools were only about eight miles apart.

Mack pounded her glove. "C'mon, Halie. Fire it in there."

Halie threw a first pitch strike to the Seagulls' big catcher. The fans cheered, Mack included.

"Another one," Mack called from center.

"Strike two," the home plate umpire yelled.

Mack figured that Halie was going to throw her change-up next, and sure enough Halie fumbled with the ball in her glove, pointed her elbow toward third base, and slowed down her delivery. The batter wasn't fooled by the pitch and ripped a shot down the left field line.

Mack watched in horror as the steaming line drive bounced fair and careened all the way to the fence. By the time Taylor threw the ball back to the infield, the Seagulls had scored three runs and the batter stood winded on third base.

"C'mon, Halie," Mack muttered under her breath as she trotted back to her position.

By the time the top of the first inning was over, the Seagulls were ahead by a score of 6-0.

Mack led off batting for her team, but got into trouble early. She tried to bunt for a hit twice, but fouled off both pitches. With two strikes on her, she had to swing away. The Seagull pitcher, unlike Halie, had a very deceptive off-speed pitch, and Mack struck out swinging.

She hung her head and slinked back to the dugout, dragging her bat behind her.

"Sorry, guys. Pick me up, Ashley."

But Ashley didn't pick her up, nor did Marci. The Seagulls' pitcher struck them both out.

Mack sprinted out to center field imagining she was Caitlin Lowe and that Jessica Mendoza sprinted to left and Laura Berg to right.

Lowe, Mendoza, and Berg along with the rest of Team USA were, like, the gods of softball. They were the best of the best and not just the best in the United States. They were the best softball players in the entire world. And if Jupiter and Mars had teams, Mack bet that Team USA could beat them, too. Unless they had some kind of weird gravity thing going on, then that might prove a little challenging.

"C'mon, Henry," Taylor yelled from left field and then laughed for Mack's benefit.

Mack put a hand over her mouth so she wouldn't laugh out loud. Taylor had picked up on the fact that Halie and Mack were like the IOC and Team USA. They didn't like each other very much. Well, except for lately. Halie had almost been nice to Mack since she got back on the team. Well, Halie wasn't exactly friendly, but at least she wasn't mean like usual.

Halie let up three base hits in a row, the last of which scored another run for the Seagulls. Coach Parks called time out and walked to the circle. Mack hadn't ever been in a game when the coach came out to talk to the pitcher. She wasn't sure what she was supposed to do, so she motioned for Taylor and Marci to join her in center field.

As soon as they reached her, Mack cringed. "Oh, no, you guys, Coach is taking Halie out of the game."

They watched Halie fume off the field and fling her glove into the dugout in disgust.

"Henry's upset," Taylor said, stating the uber obvious.

"Look, here comes Kristina." Mack pointed to the dugout.

"To save the day, I hope," Marci said.

Once Kristina finished her warm up pitches, the outfielders did their standard stick-together cheer and ran back to their positions. Mack hoped her team could turn the game around.

Thankfully Kristina didn't allow the Seagulls to score any more runs. Unfortunately for the Hawks, the Seagulls' pitcher was way too much for them, and they were shut out by a score of 0-7.

Taylor kicked the dirt after the high-five line. "I can't believe we lost to the stupid Seagulls."

"I know." Mack didn't know what else to say because she figured Halie felt bad enough as it was. Halie didn't put her gear away with everyone else. She sulked on the end of the bench, staring blankly into space. Someone, Mack wasn't sure who, had retrieved Halie's thrown glove and placed it on the bench next to her, but Mack didn't think Halie had even touched it.

"C'mon, dude," Ashley said. "Why so slow? You're usually a jack rabbit."

"Go ahead, Ash. I'll be there in a sec."

Ashley shrugged and walked out with Taylor and Marci.

Mack wasn't sure why she was going to do what she was about to do. She sat on the bench as close to Halie as she dared, which was kind of like getting close to the alligators they brought out at the Black Hammock restaurant. She never knew if the gator was going to lunge at her or not. Of course, at the Black Hammock they used duct tape to hold the gator's mouth shut. Halie had no such tape.

"Uh, Halie?"

Halie didn't respond and didn't even turn to look at her.

"I'm sorry Coach pulled you out of the game, but, um, I noticed something in batting practice one time. About your change-up."

Halie sat as still as a stone statue.

"Um, you have a *tell*." Mack made air-quotes around the word tell. "That's a poker term. My dad taught it to me when we played Texas Hold 'Em. Anyway, I can try to help you if you want."

Halie turned her head slowly and stared at Mack.

Mack swallowed hard at the expression in Bag o' Chip's gator eyes.

"Go read a comic book and leave me alone," Halie said way too calmly.

"But I just—"

"You're not even a pitcher, so go jump." Halie grabbed her bag and bolted out of the dugout.

Mack sighed and picked up Halie's glove. She put it in her bag for safe keeping even though most of her wanted to just leave the thing on the bench to rot or get stolen, but a small part of her, a part she didn't quite understand, wouldn't let her do that.

Chapter 21

Help Me

Mack sat with Ashley, Taylor, and Marci on the Winterford High School bleachers. Coach Parks had them wear their orange uniform jerseys so the high school team would know the middle school team was there rooting for them. Mack loved that their entire Wednesday practice was devoted to watching the high school team's game against Doddwood.

Taylor nudged Mack. "Hey, Rook. Way to go three for four yesterday."

"Thanks. I'm just glad we finally beat the Owls."

"Yeah, but two and three is still a losing record."

"But like Coach said," Ashley added, "there's a lot of season left so we have time to turn it around."

Taylor nodded. "I hope so."

They stood up when the tinny PA system blared the national anthem. The Winterford Tigers took off their black and orange visors and held them over their hearts. Mack followed their example and took off the Stanford University visor she'd decided to wear that day. She sang the anthem silently to herself.

The Tigers' pitcher started her warm up pitches.

"Look how fast she throws," Mack said. "How are we ever going to hit that in high school?"

"You'd better start praying for me now," Taylor said with a panicked expression. "That's going to be me next year."

Mack, Ashley, and Marci laughed, which caught the attention of Halie and her Chipettes. Mack did her best to ignore them when they pointed and laughed at her and her friends.

"Dude, what is their problem?" The irritation in Ashley's voice was obvious.

Mack sighed. "I don't know. Just ignore them."

"Whatever," Ashley muttered. Halie and her Chipettes pointed and laughed once more. Ashley added under her breath, "Jerks."

Taylor and Marci giggled at Ashley's outburst and then refocused on the game. Everything about the game was quicker and faster than their middle school games. Every player moved on every play, either fielding the ball or backing up a base. If the ball was hit to the shortstop, the right fielder backed up first base in case of an overthrow. And every player, including the Tigers' pitcher and catcher, ran on and off the field.

Coach Parks turned around. "Girls, watch the player that plays your position. Try to learn from them."

Mack watched the center fielders from both teams while Ashley remained riveted by the second basemen.

"Dude, did you see that girl dive? I want to do that. You've got to show me how."

"Me? I dove once and it was an accident. I couldn't get my feet back under me."

"Yeah, right, Rook," Taylor said with disbelief. "It looked kind of perfect to me."

"Yeah, well, it wasn't."

"You have to show us how to dive," Marci said.

Mack shrugged. "When I figure it out, I'll let you know."

"Fair enough," Marci said.

The Winterford Tigers had a winning tradition and that day was no exception. They were up early in the game and kept the lead through five innings without letting the Doddwood Dragons score a single run. In the top of the sixth inning, the Dragons managed to get a runner all the way to third base, but with two outs it looked doubtful they would score. The Dragons batter fouled off the first two pitches, but on the third pitch hit a pop up just over the second baseman's head. Mack groaned with the rest of the fans. She was sure the ball would drop in for a base hit, and the Dragons would score their first run, costing the Tiger pitcher her shut-out. The Tiger right fielder must have had other ideas, though, because she ran in and did something so amazing that Mack's jaw dropped open. The right fielder, running at full speed, slid feet first on the outfield grass and caught the pop up about six inches from the ground. Mack and her friends leaped to their feet and cheered wildly.

She replayed the slide in her mind over and over and realized it was just like sliding into second base or something, but with a glove on your hand. She could do that.

"That was awesome." Taylor smacked Mack on the arm.

"Who do we play next?" Mack asked excitedly.

"The mighty Saints from Tuskford," Ashley said.

"Let's dive like that against them."

Marci looked like a deer caught in the headlights. "Guys, I can't do that."

Taylor laughed. "Yeah, actually, I'm kind of with you. We'll let Rookie do it first, okay?"

"Okay," Marci said with obvious relief.

Mack watched the high school players on the field and felt like she was a part of something big. Something dyslexia and Mrs. Hendricks weren't ever going to keep her from again. She felt good about that for a moment until she remembered that the IOC had cut softball out of the Olympics. Her heart ached at the thought.

"Guys," she blurted, "what are we going to do when they take softball out of the Olympics? Where are we going to play after college?"

"Way to bum us out, Rook."

"Sorry, but it just stinks."

"Yeah, it does." Taylor nodded.

"We'll play in the NPF. We could all be on the same team," Ashley said.

"What's the NPF?" Marci asked.

"The National Pro Fastpitch League," Ashley said. "They have, like, six teams now, but by the time we're out of college they'll have a hundred and six."

"That'd be nice," Mack said, "but major league baseball doesn't even have that many."

"Whatever, but we all have to play on the same team, okay?" Ashley insisted.

"What are the teams?" Taylor asked.

"Oh, uh, let's see. There's the Akron Racers, that's in Ohio somewhere. The Philadelphia Force, the New England Riptide, Washington Glory, and . . . wait, how many is that so far?"

"Four," Marci said. "You need two more."

"Rockford Thunder," Mack added proudly. "That's where Cat Osterman plays."

"Yup," Ashley said. "Oh, and the Chicago Bandits where Jennie Finch is."

"How come Florida doesn't have a team?" Taylor asked.

They cheered when the Tigers got another base hit.

"My mom told me we used to have a pro softball team in Orlando," Ashley said. "The Wahoos or something, and Crystl Bustos played on it, but it didn't last long."

"What's a wahoo?" Marci asked with raised eyebrows. "I like our team name, the Hawks. I'd hate to be a Wahoo. Can you imagine? People would cheer, 'Whoo-hoo, go Wahoos!' It's just weird."

"I think a wahoo is some kind of fish or something," Taylor said. "Don't ask me how I know that, but you're right, Hawks is a way better name. In high school, we get to be the Tigers."

"I'm going to play for the Thunder after college," Mack declared, "but what I really want is to play on the Olympic team."

"Me, too," Taylor agreed.

"Me, three," Ashley and Marci chimed in at the same time. They both said, "Jinx," and laughed.

Taylor put her hand out face up and the others put theirs face down on top. "On three. One, two, three."

"Stick together," they said, but not too loudly. The game was still going on, and they didn't want to draw too much attention to themselves.

Coach Parks smiled at them and then turned back to watch the game.

The visiting Dragons were trying to get a base runner in the top of the seventh inning with two outs, but their last batter popped up in the infield. The Tigers' pitcher got under it for the third out saving her own shut-out.

Mack and her friends stood up and clapped at the high school team's win. They made their way off the bleachers and walked around the high school soccer field toward the middle school. Halie dropped back from her friends to walk next to Mack.

"What do you want?" Ashley said.

"For you to mind your own business. Go on." She waved Ashley away. "I want to talk to Mack." Ashley didn't move. "Alone."

Ashley raised an eyebrow at Mack.

Mack shrugged. "It's okay, I'll catch up with you guys later."

"The other day you said something," Halie said, once Ashley, Taylor, and Marci were out of ear shot.

"Yeah?"

"About my change-up."

Mack wasn't sure what Halie was up to, but she didn't want to be made fun of again by Halie and her Chipettes. "What about it?"

"Help me." Halie spoke so quietly that Mack wasn't sure she had actually said anything.

Mack waited for Halie to add some kind of rude remark for the benefit of her Chipettes, but she didn't and Mack realized Halie was dead serious.

Chapter 22

Unspoken Truce

Suzanne, the team's catcher and official Chipette, stayed late after practice to help Mack work on Halie's pitching. Mack stood in the batter's box and correctly guessed each one of Halie's pitches well before it reached the plate.

Halie stamped a foot in the dirt, creating a cloud of dust. "How are you doing that?"

Mack watched the dust settle on the grass and chose her words carefully. "Well, uh, I think it's the way you present the ball." She went on to explain each of Halie's tells, including the uber-obvious change-up.

"I never knew I did those things," Halie said.

"I'm not a pitcher," Mack said, "but if you could maybe make all your windups and deliveries look like your fast ball, that would help."

"I'll try," Halie said with uncertainty.

Mack, Halie, and Suzanne continued to stay after practices and after a while Halie got pretty good at disguising not only her change-up but the rest of her pitches, too. Coach Parks always watched them from a distance, but never interfered. Mack figured Coach wanted to let them work it out on their own.

Mack became a lot more relaxed around Halie during their after-practice practices. An unspoken truce had developed between them, which could have been the start of a friendship—she wasn't sure—but at least Halie wasn't making fun of her anymore.

At their last session together before spring break, Mack and Halie walked toward the gym together. Suzanne had already gone home.

Halie cleared her throat. "Mack?"

"Yeah?"

"Can I ask you a question?"

"Okay."

"Why are you helping me?"

Mack stopped walking so Halie did, too. They looked at each other for a long time. "I just thought I could. Why shouldn't I help you?"

Halie snorted. "Because I've been such a bee-otch to you."

"Oh, yeah, there's that."

Halie looked down and murmured, "I'm sorry."

"I *can* read, you know. I have a B- in English now." Mack couldn't help the accusatory tone in her voice, especially since Halie had brought the whole subject up.

"I know. I'm sorry. I, uh . . ." Halie hesitated as if trying to figure out how to say something that was difficult for her. "My shrink says I have issues."

Mack had never heard of a sixth grader going to a psychiatrist. "I didn't know you went to a shrink."

Halie glanced at Mack. "Yeah, my mom makes me. She and Dr. Buhler say I lash out at people because I'm not adjusting to my parents' divorce or something. Whatever." She flicked her hand in dismissal.

"I'm sorry."

"That's okay. My dad moved out in September. He lives with his secretary. My mom calls her the bimbo. I think it's hilarious."

They walked toward the gym in silence for a while.

"Do you ever get to see him?" Mack asked.

"Sometimes, but it's a real chore for him."

"If you ever want to talk about it, you can talk to me, I guess."

Halie shrugged. "Thanks. I probably have to figure this out on my own, though." She walked to her mom's car and then turned around and waved. "See you tomorrow."

Mack was dazed. Halie had actually apologized.

Chapter 23

Jamie Gray

Spring break was the best invention ever, Mack decided. The FCAT tests were over, and she thought she'd done well on both the reading and math sections. And since school was on break, she didn't have to go to classes, but softball went on as usual. Her team had even gone on a winning streak during the past two weeks. They beat the Tuskford Saints and the Pinegrove Lions and then they beat the Redlake Pirates again which gave them a winning record.

Earlier that day, their comfortable record was marred when they lost again to their arch-rivals, the Jamestown Seagulls, making their overall record five wins and four losses.

Mack sat in her room reading from her history book. Even though it was spring break, her parents insisted she get ahead in her schoolwork, so she sifted through the textbook and used her computer to look up unfamiliar words. Her mom had found this cool dictionary.com website that not only defined the words, but let her hear how they were pronounced. Now she didn't have to bug her parents or Mrs. Perez for the pronunciation all the time.

She worked on her words, trying not to stay bummed out about the loss to the stupid Seagulls earlier in the day, but she couldn't help it. That, of course, made her think about Olympic softball getting voted out in 2012. She decided that a quick study break wouldn't hurt and typed "Olympic Softball" into her search engine. A ton of websites came up. She'd been to a few of them before, including usasoftball.com, but the listing directly underneath that one caught her eye. The heading read, "Please help save olympic softball! Sign our online petition!" She didn't hesitate and clicked on the link which took her to a website called savesoftball.com.

Staring at her from the screen was a picture of Jamie Gray, a fourteen-year-old girl from Delray Beach, Florida, who had a quote on her website which said, "Some how, some way, some day, I will represent my country, and play fast-pitch softball for TEAM USA in the World Olympics."

Mack realized she was holding her breath. Jamie Gray's website could have been her own, because that was exactly how she felt. Her hands were shaking as she moved the mouse pointer over the yellow softball. Underneath the ball it said, "Click on the ball to sign my petition. HELP SAVE OLYMPIC SOFTBALL."

Mack clicked on the softball, and an electronic petition popped up. There were spots to enter her name, address, and email. Under that she could leave comments. She scrolled down and saw some of the comments other people had written. All kinds of people left comments—moms and dads, girls her age, older girls, and even some boys. She was amazed to discover messages from all around the world. People wrote in from places like the Netherlands, England, Spain, China, Japan, and so many more.

She couldn't contain herself any longer.

"Mom," she yelled. She leaped from her chair and called out the open door toward the living room. "Mom. Dad. You gotta come here. I found something."

She heard her mom's footsteps in the hall first followed quickly by her dad's.

"Did a lizard get in the house?" her mom said.

"No. Come see what I found. This is perfect."

Mack scurried back to her desk and sat down. She waited for her parents to stand behind her.

"Oh, Mack. Have you been online instead of studying?"

"No, Mom. I really was doing my homework. See?" She pointed to her open history book and the list of vocabulary words in her notebook. "I took a study break to look up Olympic softball. Look what I found." She pointed eagerly at the screen.

"Save softball dot com," her dad said. "Very cool."

"This girl's trying to get people to sign her petition. She's a catcher. Can we fill it out? Please?" Mack pleaded. "You told me never to fill in anything that asked for my address and stuff, so can you guys do it?"

Her dad leaned over and reached for the mouse to navigate around the website. He looked at her mom. "This looks fine. Let's do it."

Her mom nodded, and Mack bolted out of the chair to let her dad sit. He typed in Mack's name and the other information. "Okay, what do you want to say in the comments?"

"Oh, uh, I don't know." Mack wanted it to be perfect. She wanted the IOC members to read her comment and feel so bad that they'd reinstate softball instantly, without even a vote.

Her mom leaned in and read some of the other people's comments. "How about we list all the countries playing softball in this year's Olympics and make a case not only for the United States, but for all those other countries as well."

"Sounds good," her dad said. "Sound okay to you, Stinky?"

"Yeah. I know all the teams by heart so start typing. Ready?"

He nodded.

"Australia, Canada, China, Japan, the Netherlands, Chinese Taipei, Venezuela, and the United States of America. Don't just put USA, okay? Type out the words." She wanted the IOC to take a few extra seconds reading her country's name.

Her dad added another comment explaining how young girls dreamed of competing for their countries in the Olympics and that, even though the petition was started in the United States of America, it affected girls and women in countries all over the world.

Something else popped into her head. "Dad?"

"Yes?"

"Jessica Mendoza and Natasha Watley went to South Africa. They did all these free softball clinics there. If we put that in, that'll show that lots of other countries are interested in softball, too."

"Great idea." Her dad added Mack's new idea and then hit the sign button to send their comments.

"We need to get everybody to sign this petition," Mack said thoughtfully. "We have to make posters with the website on it and hang them up at games. Like on Saturday."

"Great idea," her mom said. "And we can make smaller flyers with the website on it to hand out. That way they'll—"

"Can we make the flyers right now?" Mack jumped up and down and grinned at her parents.

Her mom frowned. "Tomorrow, after your practice."

Her dad stood up. "I think you need to get back to your studies right now."

Outwardly Mack frowned and slumped back down at her desk, but inside she was excited. Maybe she actually could help Jamie Gray save Olympic softball after all.

Mack and her parents walked toward the softball field for Saturday's game against the Orangeville Owls. She saw Ashley and ran over to her. "Do you have your posters? Here are mine." She held out the two big posters she had made using permanent markers.

"Yeah, my mom has them, and Taylor and Marci have theirs, too. We have to hang them everywhere."

"Even on the concession stand, if they'll let us."

"Dude, of course, they'll let us. We should put the little flyers there, too."

"I'll get some from my mom. I can't believe we only have until October 2009 to change that Olympic committee's mind."

"I know. The 2016 Olympics are, like, eight years away but we don't have much time to convince them."

"I know. I thought we had a lot more time. Oh, hey, did you get the rocks?"

Ashley laughed. "Yeah, my mom has them in her purse."

"In her purse?"

"She keeps everything in there."

"Cool. I'll tell my mom."

Mack ran back to her parents. She wished they would hurry up. She had to get ready for the game, but she wanted to hang up all the posters and put the stacks of flyers on both sets of bleachers and the concession stand first. The rocks in Ashley's mom's purse were the weights to hold the flyers down so they wouldn't blow all over the place.

Mack looked thoughtfully at her parents. "I hope people go to the website and sign the petition."

Her dad smiled sympathetically. "I think they will. It's extremely easy."

"And," her mom added, "who wouldn't want to save softball in the Olympics? Unless some evil IOC members are here."

Mack squinted and looked around. Her parents laughed, and she realized they were kidding. "Cut it out, you guys."

Chapter 24

Arch Rivals

Three weeks after Mack and her friends put up the savesoftball.com posters and handed out flyers for the first time, Mack stood in center field of the Jamestown Middle School softball field. The Hood Hawks were playing the Redlake Pirates in the semi-final round of the season-ending tournament.

She pounded her glove. "C'mon, Kristina. Fire it in there."

If her team got one more out, they'd beat the third place Pirates and play in the league championship game against their arch-rivals, the Jamestown Seagulls who had a perfect 16-0 record. Even though the Seagulls had come in first place during the regular season, they could still lose their title if Mack's second place Hawks' team beat them in the next game.

"Strike three. That's the ball game," the umpire said.

Mack jumped high in the air in celebration and then joined her teammates storming Kristina in the pitcher's circle. They smothered her in a giant group hug and then made their way to the dugout.

"Okay, girls, settle down," Coach Parks said.

It was hard, but Mack and her teammates calmed down as best they could.

"The Seagulls have had over an hour to rest since beating the fourth place Owls," Coach Parks said. "We've had no rest. So if you feel tired, find your reserve. Dig deep. We need to be firing on all cylinders if we want to show them who's the better team." She looked at Mack. "Outfield?"

Mack snapped to attention.

"You are on notice. This team will run on you, so get to the ball quickly and don't hesitate when you throw it back in."

Mack, Taylor, and Marci looked at each other and nodded in solidarity. They knew what this game meant.

"Infielders," Coach Parks continued, "be ready to throw to a base if you're taking a relay from the outfield and be ready to put the tag on every runner."

Mack hadn't been nervous during the first game—not really—but her stomach started to knot up. She took a deep breath and made the mistake of looking at the Seagulls dugout. They were laughing and joking around, but still looked confident and sure of themselves. Being undefeated probably did that to a team.

Coach Parks put a hand on Kristina's shoulder."How are you feeling, kiddo? Are you up for another one?"

Kristina flexed her arm. "I feel good, Coach. I can do it."

"Okay, you'll start," Coach Parks turned to Halie, "but I want you to get warmed up with Suzanne and be ready to go in the game at a moment's notice. Okay?"

Halie's eyes widened. "Okay, Coach."

Mack heard the uncertainty in Halie's voice. The Seagulls were the team they'd been playing when Halie got yanked out of the game in the second inning earlier in the season. Halie probably didn't want to recreate that memory.

Mack stepped into the batter's box ready for the first pitch of the championship game against the Jamestown Seagulls. The Seagulls' pitcher took the sign from her catcher and started her windup. Mack took her steps and dropped the bat down to bunt. She pulled it back when the ball landed in the dirt. The first and third baseman took giant steps toward home, obviously expecting her to bunt again on the next pitch. The pitcher started her windup, and the third baseman crept even closer to the plate. Mack slapped the ball just beyond her reach.

Safe at first base, she took a deep breath to calm her nerves. She looked to Coach Parks for the signs as Ashley stepped up to bat. Coach wanted Mack to steal on the second pitch if Ashley didn't hit the ball on the first pitch.

Mack sprinted off the base as if she were going to steal second, but stopped close enough to first base in case she had to dive back.

The catcher didn't throw, but was up on her feet ready to. The Seagulls' catcher was an eighth grader who was one of the best, if not *the* best, catcher in the whole league. Coach Parks told them she wouldn't be surprised if their catcher went straight to varsity as a ninth grader. Coach Parks also told them they wouldn't be stealing many bases against her.

The Seagulls pitcher started her windup for the second pitch and as she released the ball, Mack exploded toward second base. She knew she had a good jump. Her teammates yelled for her to slide and she did, right into the waiting glove of the shortstop.

"Out," the umpire yelled.

Mack smacked the ground and jumped up. She ran back to the visitor's dugout.

"It was close, kiddo. You were flying," Coach Parks said.

Mack nodded and sat on the bench. She rarely got caught stealing, and it wasn't a good feeling.

"That was close, Rookie," Taylor said.

"I thought you were safe," Halie said.

"Thanks." Mack knew she had been tagged out fair and square, but thought it was kind of cool that Halie was being friendly.

She turned her attention back to the game just in time to see Ashley strike out.

"That's okay, Ash. You'll get 'em next time."

Ashley put her bat in the rack and took off her helmet. "Dude, that pitcher is crazy fast."

"I know. Their whole stupid team is good."

"That's why they're undefeated."

"Yeah." Mack heard the defeat in her own voice even though she was trying to stay positive.

"C'mon, Marci. Base hit."

Marci grounded out to the pitcher to end the Hawks chances of scoring in the first inning.

Mack grabbed her trusty Cat Osterman glove and sprinted out to center field. She pounded her glove as the first Seagull batter got up to bat.

"Ninety miles an hour, Kristina. C'mon, pitcher."

She bent her knees, ready to sprint in any direction. The first batter smacked a single just out of Ashley's reach. Mack scooped up the ball and tossed it back to Ashley on second base.

Mack smacked her glove again as the next batter got up. "C'mon, Kristina. C'mon, fourteen. Fire it in there."

The batter put down a sacrifice bunt. Tonya, The Hawks third baseman, charged in and threw the ball to first, but the runner flew down the line and stepped on the base a split second before the ball got there. Taylor snuck in from left field to cover third and glared at the runner on second as if daring her to try and advance.

The Seagulls had runners on first and second with no outs. Mack prayed for the infield to turn a double play or something, but the third Seagulls' batter of the inning smashed a line drive hitting Kristina somewhere on the leg.

Kristina howled in pain as she fell to the ground. Despite her obvious injury, the play went on. Suzanne ran toward the pitcher's circle. She was obviously torn between helping Kristina and making sure the runner on third didn't run home. She grabbed the ball and backpedaled to home plate. Thankfully, the runner held at third.

Suzanne held the ball in the air.

"Time," the umpire said and held up both arms.

Coach Parks ran out to Kristina, who sat clutching her left shin. The infielders created a crowd around their fallen pitcher. The outfielders joined Mack in center field.

Mack wasn't sure what had happened to Kristina, but blew out a frustrated sigh when Coach Parks and Suzanne created a chair with their arms and carried Kristina off the field.

Ashley turned around to Mack, Taylor, and Marci. "She got hit right on the shinbone. The bump is this big." She indicated a golf ball sized lump. "It's gross."

"I hope she's okay," Mack said.

"Yeah, really," Taylor added. "She's done for the day, I guess."

Sure enough, Halie walked out of the dugout and into the pitcher's circle. Taylor and Marci went back to their positions, and Mack practically held her breath as Halie took her five warm up pitches. Bases loaded with no outs. It was going to be a long game.

Chapter 25

Go For It

Mack pounded her glove. "C'mon, Halie, you can do this."

Halie turned around, looked at Mack, and bugged her eyes out as if to say she wasn't so sure she could, especially with no outs and the bases loaded.

Mack could only imagine the kind of pressure Halie was under. "You're in charge two-seven. You can do this."

Halie pressed her lips tighter in resolve, nodded back, and turned around to face the batter.

The Seagulls' catcher dug her heels in the batter's box. Coach Parks motioned for the outfielders to take a few steps back because their catcher could clear the bases with one swing. Oh, yeah, kind of like she did the last time Halie pitched to her with the bases loaded.

Halie threw her first pitch.

"Strike one," the umpire yelled.

"Keep it going, two-sev, keep it going," Mack yelled.

The batter fouled the next pitch off behind the plate.

"Two strikes for you, pitch," Mack called. "One more now."

The batter swung and missed Halie's now ultra sneaky change-up for strike three and the first out of the inning.

Halie turned around to face Mack sporting a wide grin. Mack smiled back and threw her a thumbs-up. "Do it again, pitcher. You've got the stuff."

"C'mon, Halie," Ashley yelled from second base.

Mack was happy to hear Ashley and the rest of the team cheering for Halie. Halie had been a lot friendlier to everybody lately, including Ashley.

The Hawks weren't out of danger yet because the bases were still loaded with only one out. The next Seagulls' batter stepped in the box and arrogantly looked toward the outfield as if trying to find the holes and gaps. She swung on the first pitch and popped the ball up just over the shortstop out of reach. Mack sprinted in with all her might. On the run, she made a split-second decision to do something she'd never done before. She prayed that Taylor and Marci backed her up, just in case it didn't work.

She tried to time it right as she slid feet first on the outfield grass. The ball landed in her glove on the fly inches from the ground. With her teammates cheering, she used the momentum from the slide to pop back up on her feet. The third base runner was desperately trying to get back to the base. Mack heaved the ball to Tonya.

"Out at third," the umpire yelled.

Mack leaped in the air, ran to Tonya, and hugged her.

Mack pulled back from the hug. "I was praying you were ready 'cause I was coming up throwing somewhere to somebody."

"I was ready. I'm just glad you looked here first."

Mack, Halie, and Tonya got mobbed by their teammates in the dugout.

"Dude, that was awesome." Ashley hugged Mack. She turned to Halie. "Nice pitching."

Halie looked surprised that Ashley had actually spoken to her. "Thanks, Ash."

"Way to get out of that one, girls, but we've got a new inning to tackle so let's stay focused," Coach Parks said. "We have to think of each inning as its own mini-game. I'm proud of you for not letting them win that first inning, but let's go out and win the second one."

"Maybe those Seagulls won't think this is just another stroll on the beach. Right, dude?" Ashley said.

Mack took a deep breath. "Here's hoping."

The Hawks still couldn't find a way to unlock the secrets of the Seagulls' pitcher, and didn't score any runs. The Seagulls couldn't unlock Halie's pitches, either, so the score remained tied at 0-0 going into the seventh inning.

Stephanie, the first Hawk's batter of the top of the seventh inning, struck out. Mack stepped up to bat. The first and third basemen came way in clearly expecting a bunt. The pitcher started her windup, and Mack noticed the first baseman drift back toward her base. She gently tapped a bunt up the first base line, threw on her after burners, and blasted to first base. The pitcher fielded the bunt and threw to first, but Mack beat the throw.

Ashley stepped up to the plate and Coach Parks flashed the signs. Steal. Mack rocked on the base and took off for second on the pitch. She slid hard into the base, creating a cloud of dust. This time the catcher's throw was high, and Mack was safe.

"Way to go, Mack," Marci yelled from the on-deck circle.

Mack heard her parents cheering from the stands, but she couldn't think about them because she had to figure out a way to get to third base.

She remembered something she'd seen at the Winterford High School game. If it didn't work, Coach Parks and the whole team would probably stay mad at her forever, but if it did work . . .

Mack took a deep breath and readied herself. She was going to try and steal third base, even though no one on the Hawks' team had dared try. The Seagulls' catcher was too good. Coach always told them to explode off the base as if they were going to steal the next base, but Mack took a leisurely four or five steps off second base on the first pitch. And just as she hoped, the catcher didn't even look at her and lobbed the ball back to the pitcher from her knees. The instant the ball left the catcher's hand, Mack sprinted for third base. Both sides of the field erupted. She kept her head low and prayed. She slid in feet first and waited for the call.

No call came, so she jumped to her feet.

"Their pitcher froze. She didn't throw over," Coach Parks said. "Mackenzie Kelly, do you mind telling me how you learned to delay steal? You gave me a heart attack."

"Sorry, Coach." Mack grinned. "One of the high school players did that in the game you took us to."

"Okay, then." Coach Parks smiled and shook her head. "This changes things now that you're on third."

Coach Parks asked for time and spoke to Ashley who had been the batter the entire time Mack was merrily stealing bases.

Ashley's eyes widened and she nodded to Coach Parks. Mack had no idea what was going on until Coach Parks gave the signs. She gulped. No wonder Ashley was nervous. Coach just called for the suicide squeeze.

Although they had worked on the squeeze play during practice, they had never used it during an actual game. Mack was supposed to sprint home as soon as the pitch left the pitcher's hand, and Ashley, who had the harder job, needed to bunt the ball onto the field making certain it hit the ground. Ashley would need to bunt the very next pitch, even if it was in the dirt or over her head, otherwise Mack would be a sitting duck at home plate.

Mack took a deep breath while the pitcher took the signal from the catcher. The pitcher wound up and let go. Mack leaped off the base toward home and didn't stop. She now understood why it was called a suicide play. *C'mon, Ashley, c'mon.*

Ashley squared around. She bent low to reach the ball at ankle height. She made contact, and the ball rolled onto the field toward the first base line.

Stay fair! Mack hollered in her head. It did. The charging first baseman picked up the ball, and to Mack's amazement stopped to tag out Ashley before throwing home. Mack slid. The catcher tagged her on the hip.

It seemed like an eternity, but the umpire finally yelled, "Safe."

Mack leaped in the air and then hugged Ashley. The Hawk fans cheered and stomped their feet. Her teammates pounded her helmet as she tried to get in the dugout.

"Rookie, you're my idol." Taylor pulled Mack into a bear hug.

"Cut it out," Mack said with a grin. "Aren't you on-deck?"

"Oh, yeah. See ya."

Even though the dugout quieted down, Mack still felt the excited energy of her teammates.

Halie sat down next to her. "I don't know how you do that."

"Do what?"

"You just go for it. Stealing bases, diving for balls in the outfield. You're not afraid."

Mack thought about it for a second and remembered something Mrs. Perez said to her when she complained about all the new study techniques.

"Nothing ventured, nothing gained. I'm just glad I was safe when I tried that delay steal because everybody would have hated me if I got called out, but you know what?"

"What?"

"I'd hate myself more for not trying."

Halie smiled. "I'm glad we're on the same team."

"Me, too." Mack stood up to get her glove after Marci popped out to end the top of the seventh inning. "And now it's your turn to go for it. Three outs and we're the champions."

The Hawks ran out onto the field not looking like they had played thirteen innings of softball in a row on a humid Florida afternoon. Halie struck out the first batter of the inning. The next batter tried to slap the ball past Ashley, but she fielded the grounder on the run for the second out. Mack felt her knees get wobbly as the third batter of the inning stepped into the batter's box. The batter fouled off the first two pitches, and Mack figured Halie would throw her sneaky change-up. The batter wasn't fooled, though, and made solid contact with the pitch. The ball sailed into left field. The Hawks were in trouble.

"Taylor, it's you. It's you," Mack shouted. "Go school, school."

Taylor was already in motion.

"School, school," Mack yelled louder, her voice echoing off the school building.

Taylor adjusted her path slightly toward the Jamestown Middle School building. She looked up just as the ball started to sail over her head. Like a Tampa Bay Bucs wide receiver, she reached up over her shoulder and snatched the ball out of the air.

"Whoo hoo," Mack yelled. She u-turned and jumped on Taylor in celebration. "You did it," Mack yelled in Taylor's face. "We won." Taylor let her down, and Mack threw her Cat Osterman glove high in the air.

The rest of the Hawks' team stormed them in left field. They had just done the impossible. They had taken down the giant, their undefeated rivals, and stolen the championship trophy right out of their hands.

Mack pulled herself out of the celebration pile. She knew now, more than ever, that if it felt this good to win a middle school championship, she just had to find a way to play for Team USA in the Olympics.

Chapter 26

Conference USA

Mack tapped the eraser end of her pencil on the worksheet, and then put her head down on the dining room table.

"C'mon, Mack," Halie said. "Those vocabulary words aren't going to define themselves."

Mack groaned. "I know, but the game's on in a little while, and I can't concentrate."

"Hey," Halie said with a smile, "the dealio we made with your parents was that I'd help you for an hour with English before we watched the game."

Mack picked her head up and rolled her eyes. "Okay, okay, but we have five more minutes and then that's it."

"Okay, but tomorrow we're working on spelling. Just so you know."

Mack groaned and slammed open the dictionary to look up the word "catharsis."

"Catharsis means to get relief from your pent-up emotions. What the heck does that mean?"

Halie laughed. "I'll give you an example. According to my shrink, my cathartic moment was when my Dad took me to Disney World, just him and me, and told me I'd always be his little girl. I know, kind of sappy, but I finally let go of the resentment I had toward him leaving. I've been dealing with things so much better since then."

"Okay, I get that."

The doorbell rang, and Mack slammed the dictionary shut. "Lesson's over. I'll get it, Mom." She ran to the door to let in Ashley, Taylor, and Marci.

"Hey, Rook," Taylor said. "Thanks for letting us watch the game at your house." She claimed a spot on the loveseat.

"No problem."

Marci sat next to Taylor. "I can't believe our parents are letting us watch the game on a school night."

Ashley smoothed down her FSU shirt. "Me, neither, but maybe since tomorrow's field day, it's okay." She was the only one not wearing a UCF Golden Knights t-shirt. She obviously wanted to stay faithful to her Florida State team.

Marci reached for a handful of potato chips from the bowl Mack's mom set on the coffee table. "If UCF beats Houston, they'll be the Conference USA champs, right?"

Everybody nodded.

"And then," Marci continued, "they go to the College World Series?"

"Yeah," Taylor said. "I'm almost going to feel bad for this Houston team when UCF knocks them out."

"Oh, dude, I know," Ashley said. "Houston's been ranked in the top twenty-five teams in the whole country all season long."

Mack found the game on the CBS sports channel. Allison Kime threw her first pitch.

"Allison Kime's so good," Ashley said in awe.

"She is," Halie agreed. "Look, there's Lindsay Dean catching for her."

"Ooh, pop up to short," Mack said. "Tiffany Lane's got it."

"One pitch, one out. I love that," Halie said.

"I bet you do," Taylor said. "Hey, look at Hillary Barrow at third and Abby McClain at second. I can't believe they're on TV."

The next Houston batter lined out to center field.

"There's your favorite player, Mack. Ashley Van Ryn," Marci said.

"I know. She's so awesome."

"C'mon, UCF," Taylor yelled at the TV. "Hold 'em."

"Yeah!" Mack squealed along with her teammates as Breanne Javier, the UCF first baseman, dove for a foul ball for the third out of the inning.

At the end of five innings, the UCF Golden Knights and the Houston Cougars were tied 2-2 with UCF coming up to bat in the top of the sixth.

"I can't wait to go to the UCF softball camp," Mack said, then turned to Taylor. "I can't believe you can't go."

"I know." Taylor sighed. "We always go to my Grandma's in New York for a few weeks when school ends."

"I wonder which UCF players will be at the camp," Ashley said.

"I hope Van Ryn is there," Mack said. "And Kime and just everybody."

Ashley's eyes bugged out. "I'm scared to meet Coach Leurs-Gillespie."

"Why?" Mack asked.

"She's got, like, over five hundred wins as a head coach, so she's probably going to expect us to be great players or something."

"You *are* great players." Taylor held up her can of orange soda in salute.

The others grabbed their beverages and saluted back.

"Maybe a Florida team will win the World Series this year," Marci said.

"The University of Florida Gators have been ranked number one, like, this whole season," Ashley said with a scowl.

"FSU fans just hate that, don't they, Ash?"

Ashley stuck out her tongue at Mack, but then laughed.

Halie leaned forward in the recliner. "Did you know that no team east of the Mississippi has ever won the World Series? Well, except Michigan in 2005."

"Yeah," Taylor said, "usually Arizona or UCLA wins, or one of those other western teams."

The top of the sixth inning started with Van Ryn up at bat. Van Ryn singled up the middle followed by Lexi Gresham, UCF's left fielder, who sacrificed her over to second.

Mack sat up excitedly. "We've got a runner in scoring position."

"Lane's up," Taylor said. "She's an awesome hitter."

"You can do it, Tiffany," Mack yelled at the television.

Lane took a big swing and smacked a homerun over the center field fence giving UCF a 4-2 lead over Houston. They leaped to their feet and cheered. Mack bumped fists with everyone and then sat down on the couch with a thump.

"Let's hope we can keep that lead." Halie sat back down.

Mack nodded in agreement.

Halie's spoken wish came true, and UCF went on to win the game for the Conference USA championship by a score of 4-2.

"When do regionals start?" Marci asked.

"This weekend," Mack said.

"So soon?" Marci sounded anxious.

"Yeah, a week before final exams. I wish the games were after the exams." Mack worried that her parents might not let her watch so much softball with final exams so close.

"Don't worry, Mack," Halie said. She put her English books in her backpack. "I'll help you study English in between innings."

"Thanks." She blew out a sigh of relief.

Chapter 27

Regionals

"We'll be in my room, Mom." Mack slammed the front door and ushered Ashley ahead of her into her room.

"Okay," her mom called. "We'll have dinner when the game's over."

"Okay."

They flung their backpacks on the unmade bed, and Mack hit the on button to her computer.

Ashley claimed Mack's desk chair. "Do you have another chair?"

"I'll get one from the office." Mack headed out the door and stopped. "Do you want a Gatorade?"

Ashley gasped. "Don't insult me. No self-respecting Seminole would ever drink something made for Gators."

Mack laughed. "Okay, I'll get waters." She rushed out the door. When she returned, Ashley had already brought up the UCF softball website.

"Dude, I can't believe the game isn't on TV."

"I know. It's not fair." Mack put two bottled waters on her desk along with a couple of boxes of raisins. She sat down in the black leather executive chair she had wheeled in from her parents' office. "Where's the Gametracker thingy?"

"Here it is." Ashley clicked on the link, and the page loaded. "Cool, dude. Look at the little cartoon field and the stick figures. Hey, there're pictures of the batter and the pitcher. Tiffany Lane's up first."

"Look at the tiny yellow ball. That's hilarious." Mack chuckled.

"And the little bat. It's so cute."

"Hey, who are they playing? It's not Florida, is it?"

"Nope," Ashley said. "It says USF. I think that's the University of South Florida in Tampa."

"How come it's only Florida teams?"

"Actually, it's not. Georgia Tech's in this regional bracket, too. My dad said teams from the same area of the country play against each other in the first round."

"Oh, look." Mack pointed to the computer screen. "It says the NCAA Gainesville Regional. Where's the Katie Seashole Pressley Softball Stadium?"

"Mack," Ashley said with a frown. "It's in Gainesville."

"Oh, duh. So the Gators have the home field advantage the whole tournament. That's kind of not fair."

"It's not," Ashley said. "Darn, we didn't score."

They laughed when the tiny white USF stick figures ran off the field.

"It's so funny watching the game this way," Mack said.

"Really." Ashley opened a box of raisins. "What stinks, though, is that only one team will make it out of this bracket alive to move on to the next round."

"And with the Gators ranked number one in the entire country, I doubt UCF'll even win one game."

By the time the top of the seventh inning rolled around, UCF was losing to Georgia Tech by a score of 1-2.

The stick figure of the UCF pitcher, Allison Kime, got up to bat with two runners on base and two outs.

Mack pointed at the screen. "One more out and we're in the loser's bracket. C'mon, Allison."

The stick figure swung the bat sending the tiny yellow ball into the air.

"Pop fly," Mack said glumly with her chin resting on her fist.

"No, it's not," Ashley yelled. "Look. It's a hit."

The ball bounced in the outfield, and Breanne Javier ran home followed quickly by Hillary Barrow. UCF was now ahead by a score of 3-2.

"We're winning, dude. I can't believe Allison Kime just hit a triple."

Mack and Ashley high-fived each other.

The UCF team held the University of South Florida scoreless in the bottom of the seventh inning and won their first ever regional contest.

"Winner's bracket, dude," Ashley yelled.

"Whoo-hoo." Mack leaped off the chair and did a happy dance in the middle of her room. She snapped to attention and got serious. "Who do we play tomorrow?"

"The winner of the University of Florida/Georgia Tech game."

"Florida," they said together and laughed.

"Can you come over tomorrow?" Mack said.

"Yeah. I love this Gametracker thing, but, um . . ."

"What?"

"Did you invite Halie, too?"

"Yeah, why?"

"I don't know." Ashley was quiet for a second. "It's just kind of weird, you know? The old Bag of Chips always made fun of us. Are you guys, like, friends now?"

"Kind of. I didn't trust her at first, but she's okay. Really."

"If you say so." Ashley didn't sound convinced.

"C'mon, Ash. You'll always be my best friend. No way, some bag o' chips is going to take your place."

"You sure?"

"For real. Halie needs some better friends than those Chipettes, anyway. And that's us."

Ashley sat taller. "Okay. I'm down with that."

"C'mon," Mack said, getting up. "Let's see if my mom can make us some victory mac and cheese."

Chapter 28

Chomped

Mack tapped the top of the flashcards. "Quiz me, Halie."

"Me, too," Ashley said.

"Okay." Halie grabbed the top index card off the stack. "Wait, what's the inning?"

Mack looked at the computer screen. "Top of the seventh. UCF's losing to the all-powerful Gators, three to nothing. Big honking surprise there."

"Let's stay positive," Ashley said.

"Okay," Halie said, "this one's for Mack. Spell and then define *allegiance*."

Mack groaned. "No way."

"C'mon, dude. You can do it," Ashley said.

"Okay." Mack took a deep breath. "Here goes. A-L-E-J-U-N-S . . . E." She smiled as she remembered to add the E at the last second.

She could tell by Halie's grimace that she'd spelled it wrong. Probably way wrong.

"Okay, you kind of spelled it the way it sounds." Halie showed Mack the word on the card. "Maybe you can just look at the whole word instead and memorize it."

Mack looked at the word and noticed the A-L-L at the beginning, the G in the middle instead of a J, and the C-E at the end. "That spelling makes no sense. See? Even the world 'sense' ends with S-E." She sighed.

"Okay, wait," Halie said. "I have an idea. Let's tape any word you misspell to the side of the computer screen. That way you'll keep seeing the words as we watch the game. Maybe your brain will take, like, little photographs of the words, and you can remember them that way."

Mack shrugged, not sure Halie's strategy would work, but she reached into the top drawer of her desk and pulled out a roll of scotch tape.

Halie taped up the word. "Okay, define it, now."

"Oh, that's easy. Allegiance means you show loyalty to something. Like our allegiance to the UCF team."

"Yeah," Ashley said as they punched fists in agreement. "Especially 'cuz my Seminoles got knocked out last night. Wah."

"Sorry, Ash. Maybe next year."

They continued to study while half-watching the losing efforts of the UCF stick figures.

Mack groaned when the UCF second baseman lined out to the Gators' third baseman to end the game.

"I hate being Gator bait," Ashley said glumly.

"That Gator pitcher chomped us good," Mack said.

Halie laughed. "Stacey Nelson? She's throws, like, crazy fast—something like sixty-eight miles an hour—and she's only a junior so she'll chomp us again next year, too."

"Oh, great." Mack moaned. "Who do we play next now that we're in the loser's bracket?"

"We have to wait for the winner of the Georgia Tech/ USF game," Ashley said, "but we won't play again until six."

"That gives us a couple hours to play catch," Mack said. "C'mon, get your gloves. Let's go out back."

They played catch in the backyard until Mack's dad gently reminded them of their deal to study. They shuffled back into her room and worked on vocabulary and spelling in addition to some reading comprehension exercises that Halie had printed from the Internet. At exactly six o'clock they tossed aside the notebooks and flashcards.

"We're playing Georgia Tech," Mack announced. "Oh, we're the visitors this time."

A wonderful aroma caught Mack's attention.

Her dad stood in the doorway holding a pizza. "Hungry, girls?"

"Yeah," they said in unison and laughed.

Mack hadn't realized how hungry she was.

"I'll bring in some Gatorades from the kitchen." He set the pizza box down. Three paper plates and napkins sat on top.

"Your family is so cool," Halie said.

Mack and Ashley exchanged a glance.

"Hey, you know you guys can come over anytime you want," Mack said.

"Thanks." Halie looked away. Mack wasn't sure, but she thought Halie brushed away a tear.

"Here you go, girls." Mack's dad handed out three red Gatorade bottles.

"Thanks, Dad."

"No problem." He left the door open a crack when he left.

"Ashley, are you going to be okay with a Gator drink?" Mack asked.

Ashley sighed dramatically. "I guess I'll have to be."

Halie and Mack laughed.

They ate their pizza, ignored their studies, and watched the UCF team score five runs in the fifth inning to give them a seven to nothing lead over the Georgia Tech Yellow Jackets. Even though the Georgia Tech team rallied in the bottom of the seventh, it wasn't enough, and UCF won the game easily.

Mack and her friends practically floated on air as they made their way to the front door. Ashley's dad waited in the car outside to drive Halie and Ashley home.

"I'll see you guys tomorrow," Mack said. "I think the game's at one. I mean, there's no way we can beat the Gators, the number one ranked team in the whole country, but we still have to show our allegiance to UCF, right?"

"Yeah," Ashley said. "See you tomorrow, dude."

"You're helping me study for math tomorrow, right?" Halie said to Mack.

Mack laughed. "It's a deal." She closed the door after them.

Chapter 29

Mercy

"Look, dude." Ashley pointed at the computer screen. "Another center fielder who bats first."

"Kim Waleszonia." Mack stumbled over the pronunciation of the University of Florida center fielder's name. "I'm glad that's not one of Mrs. Hendricks's spelling words."

"No, kidding."

They cheered when the Florida center fielder grounded out to start the game.

"Where's Halie?" Ashley asked.

"Oh, she called around noon. She had to go to her dad's."

"Oh," Ashley said quietly. "I bet she'd rather be here."

"I don't know. I think she kind of likes her dad again."

"That's good. You know what?"

"What?"

"I've decided that Halie's okay."

Mack yanked off her UCF visor and hit Ashley with it playfully. "I told you."

Ashley put her hands up in defense. "Okay, okay. So, can you help *me* with math today, instead?"

Mack laughed. "Yeah, we might as well do something productive. The Gators are going to cream us, anyway."

As Mack helped Ashley study for her math exam, they kept an eye on the stick-figure game playing on the computer screen.

"Dude," Ashley said, "it's the seventh inning and nobody's scored yet."

"Ahh," Mack whispered, "don't jinx us." She covered her ears.

"Oh, no, look." Ashley pointed to the screen. "We're going into extra innings."

"Do you think we can actually . . . ?" Mack whispered.

"Win?" Ashley finished. She looked scared. "Let's not say another word."

"Okay," Mack mouthed. She turned an imaginary key over her lips and tossed it over her shoulder.

They watched in silence but pumped their fists and stomped their feet when the Gators went down one-two-three in the top of the eighth inning.

C'mon, c'mon, c'mon, Mack cheered in her head. She punched a fist in the air when UCF got two runners on base. All they had to do was score one run and they would beat the Gators.

Ashley pointed excitedly at the screen. Allison Kime was up to bat.

Help yourself, Allison, Mack willed in her head.

Stick figure Kime swung her bat causing the tiny ball to bounce toward the Gators' second baseman. Mack held her breath, but the ball kept bouncing into the outfield. Kime was safe at first, and Lane scored the winning run from third.

Mack leaped up and shouted, "We won. We won."

"Whoo-hoo," Ashley yelled. "We beat the Gators."

Mack's parents ran into her room.

"You're kidding," her dad said. "They beat the Gators?"

Mack nodded and plopped back into the leather chair exhausted.

"That's only the Gators third loss," her dad said.

Mack steeled her chin. "And they'll get their fourth loss when we chomp them again in the next game. Can you stay, Ash?"

"Yeah, let me call my Dad." She pulled out her cell phone.

Her mom sighed. "I guess I'll order up some Chinese food."

The food was delivered fairly quickly, and Mack and Ashley ate off of TV trays in Mack's room.

Mack brushed some fallen rice off her black and gold UCF shirt. "Hey, Ash. Check out this new website I found."

Ashley put her egg roll down and grabbed the mouse. "What's the address?"

"It's called backsoftball dot com."

Ashley typed in the address. "Look, it says they want people to donate new and used softball equipment so they can send it to all kinds of countries who can't afford stuff. We have a ton of old stuff in our garage."

"Us, too. I guess they want to help the rest of the world catch up to the United States."

"Hey," Ashley said, smacking Mack on the arm, "we have to put this on our savesoftball dot com posters."

"Exactly, and I'll get my mom to put it on the flyers we're gonna hand out when summer league games start on Tuesday."

"Dude," Ashley put out a fist, "somehow, someway, we're going to get on the Olympic team in 2016." They punched fists.

"Hey, Ash, I bet I can tell you the score of the UCF-Gators game before it even starts."

"No, you can't . . . Okay, what?"

"Zero to zero."

Ashley narrowed her eyes as she thought about it. Mack smiled when realization hit Ashley's face. "Oh, I get it. The score is zero to zero *before* the game starts. Ha! Good one, dude. Who told you that?"

"My dad. Hey, Dad?" Mack called from her room. "Is the game on TV anywhere?"

"No, Stinky."

"Dad," Mack yelled making the word sound like two syllables. "Don't call me that."

"Oh, sorry, Stinky," he called back. "We've gone up and down all the channels, and we can't find the game."

Mack frowned. "Okay, thanks."

"How come nobody thinks the game is important enough to put on TV?" Ashley said. "Come on. UCF and Florida are playing. Maybe we're not big enough for ESPN or anything, but what about the Sunshine Network or that CBS College Sports channel? You'd think at least one of them would show the game."

Mack shrugged and put her hands out in a helpless gesture. "It's kind of frustrating. I mean this Gametracker thing is cool, but I want to watch the real people."

"Yeah, me, too." Ashley picked up her Gatorade. "Dude." She put the drink down quickly. "Why are we drinking Gatorade? Holy wow. We just totally jinxed the team."

"Give them to me quick," Mack said. "I'll get rid of them." She scooped up the Gatorade bottles and ushered them back to the kitchen. She came back with two bottles of water and set them on her desk.

"That was close," Ashley said.

"I know."

The Gators scored three runs in the bottom of the first inning. The Knights scored none.

The Gators continued to score run after run after run until the umpire finally ended the game by the mercy rule. The UCF Golden Knights lost to the Florida Gators by a score of 0-10.

"Dude, I can't believe we're Gator bait again."

"Yeah. The Gators were ranked number one in the whole country for a reason, I guess. UCF's season is over for a whole year," Mack said glumly.

"It was the Gatorade," Ashley said with a serious expression. "We shouldn't have had it."

"Uh, yeah. Next time we'll be drinking lemonade."

"Hey, maybe the Gators will go on to win the whole thing."

Mack raised an eyebrow in disbelief. "You're actually going to root for the Gators? You? An FSU Seminole fan?"

"I know, right? But now that UCF and FSU are out, we need a Florida team to win. That way we can say we got beat by the best."

"Okay. Hang on." Mack took her UCF visor off and replaced it with the Gators visor she had gotten for her birthday. She grinned. "Go Gators."

"I am not doing the Gator chomp."

"You have to draw the line, somewhere. Right, Ash?"

Chapter 30

Loyalty

Mack sat at her desk in Mrs. Hendrick's fourth period English class and tapped her feet. Three freshly sharpened pencils lay on her desk next to her unopened blue exam booklet.

Mrs. Hendricks cleared her throat. "Please take everything off your desk except for your blue booklet and writing instruments."

Mack took a deep breath to try and get her nerves under control. She almost laughed out loud. She was more nervous about taking this two day in-class final exam than she had been for any softball game she'd ever played in.

Mrs. Hendricks and Mrs. Perez had worked it out beforehand that Mack would write the first essay during the class period and would go to Mrs. Perez's office after school to write the second. Having extended time like that made school way easier. Mrs. Perez also got her into a two-week summer reading camp held at the high school. Mack wasn't sure about going to a camp where all she did was read, but Mrs. Perez assured her it would help with her transition to seventh grade. Since it was only two weeks and didn't interfere with the UCF softball camp, she tried not to worry about it too much.

Mack picked up a pencil and glanced back at Halie. Halie smiled and gave her a thumbs-up. Mack gave her a quick thumbs-up in return and turned back around. She felt the familiar churn of anxiety in her stomach, but forced herself to relax and stay positive. The UCF team probably felt the same way when the Gators scored run after run against them in that last game of the regional finals, but UCF never gave up. They continued to play hard, so she decided to do the same, no matter how hard the exam turned out to be.

Mrs. Hendricks picked up the stack of exams from her desk and passed them out row by row. She ripped off the second page and handed Mack the top page.

"Please begin." Mrs. Hendricks returned to sit behind her desk. Mack read the essay topic. *Write an essay describing a situation in which you showed loyalty to someone or something.*

Yes! Mack shouted in her head. She wanted to blindly start writing about softball, but slowed herself down and turned to the last page of the blue book. Mrs. Perez taught her that even though writing an outline seemed like wasted energy, organizing your thoughts really helped. With the jumble of thoughts racing through her head, she forced herself to write *Loyalty to UCF Softball* as the header. But then she thought about Cat Osterman and Coach Parks and scratched out the word *UCF*, leaving the title *Loyalty to Softball.*

Much better, she thought. Underneath the header she wrote the number one and circled it. Next to that she wrote, *Hawks Middle School Softball.* She wanted to write about how she remained loyal to the team by coming to watch games during her, hmm, how was she going to phrase it? Okay, during her leave of absence from the team. She'd write about how she practiced with her dad so she wouldn't fall too far behind. This way Mrs. Hendricks would see that playing ball wasn't a time-waster.

The next heading came easily, *UCF Softball.* She looked down at her gold UCF shirt with black writing and smiled. She would write about the billion games she, Ashley, and her parents had gone to during their season, how she and her friends watched the underdog UCF team beat nationally ranked Houston during the Conference USA championship game, and how they went on to the regional round of the College World Series. She'd point out that even though the games weren't important enough for TV stations to show, she and her friends stayed loyal and watched the games with Gametracker. And, she thought excitedly, she'd also mention the four-day UCF softball camp she, Ashley, and Halie would attend in exactly two weeks. *Only fourteen days*, she thought and squirmed in her seat. She took a deep breath and forced herself to refocus on her exam.

She calmly added the third and last heading, *Olympic Softball*. Even though she thought maybe she had enough to write about so far, it was Cat Osterman and the rest of Team USA that had sparked her interest in softball in the first place. She added an exclamation point after the heading. Of course, she'd have to include the UCF versus Team USA game at Merrill Park and how her loyalties were kind of divided that day. She'd write about the upcoming 2008 Beijing Olympics and then the lack of softball in the 2012 Olympics in London. Maybe Mrs. Hendricks would start to cry when she read how Mack and her friends made millions of posters and flyers with the backsoftball.com website and Jamie Gray's savesoftball.com website trying to get people to tell the stupid IOC know how awesome softball was. Maybe Mrs. Hendricks would even go to Jamie's website and sign the petition.

She was pleased with her outline, so she grabbed a fresh pencil and wrote and wrote and wrote. She jumped when Mrs. Hendricks said, "Five minutes left."

Mack smiled. She had one more sentence to write in her conclusion. She wrote, "My loyalty to softball is clear because of the allegiance I have shown to the Hawks middle school team, the UCF college team, and the Olympic team."

She closed her blue book and placed her three worn out pencils on top. She folded her arms and sat back satisfied that there would be no gentleman's D on this essay. No, it would be a beautiful B at least.

Chapter 31

Beijing Opening Ceremonies

Summer ticked along at a steady pace. It was August 8, 2008. The time was eight o'clock p.m. Mack wondered if Cat Osterman realized that the Olympic opening ceremony was filled with her uniform number.

Mack sat on the couch with her mom. Her dad sat in the lone recliner in the living room. She adjusted her Team USA visor and smoothed out her red, white, and blue Team USA shirt.

"Do you have your jar of lucky sharks' teeth?" her dad asked.

"Yeah, right here." Mack shook the small jar containing exactly fifteen black prehistoric sharks' teeth that she'd found when she and her family went to Venice Beach in July—one for each Team USA player. "But the softball team doesn't need the luck today. When they play their first game against Venezuela on Tuesday, that's when they need the luck."

"It's too bad the games are on in the middle of the night," her mom said. "It would be nice to watch them in primetime."

"We'll have to DVR them and watch them in the morning. Or we could . . ." Mack flashed her saddest eyes.

"No," her mom answered emphatically. "We are not staying up until two in the morning watching softball. You have school starting up in a week."

"A week and three days, Mom." Mack didn't really mind starting school again because that meant she was that much closer to softball season. Mrs. Perez warned her that seventh grade would be a tough year. She said that the odd grades, seventh, ninth, and eleventh, seemed to be the most challenging school years for students. So, although Mack was excited to no longer be a sixth grade baby, she was a little nervous about hard classes and tough teachers like Mrs. Hendricks.

"Here we go," her dad said as the commercial ended. "Let the games begin."

Mack and her parents watched in silent awe as the sights and sounds of the Chinese culture flashed on the screen.

"They just said this is China's first time hosting the Olympics," Mack said. "Is that true?"

"Apparently," her dad answered.

"Isn't China where they had that big earthquake in the spring? We gave money in homeroom for that."

"Yes," her mom said. "About five million people were left homeless."

"Five million?" Mack blinked a few times trying to grasp the number. "That's five times ten to the sixth power. I only gave five dollars. Maybe I should have given more."

They watched the colorful ceremonies unfold.

"Hey, that announcer just said the population of China is 1.3 billion, about four times as much as the entire United States, so that means," Mack did a quick calculation in her head, "the U.S. has about 325 million people. That's a lot of people."

Her parents looked at her in disbelief.

"Whose child are you?" Her dad said and then looked at her mom. "Can you calculate like that in your head?"

She shook her head. "No. Maybe they switched babies on us in the hospital." She grinned.

"Mom," Mack whined, but she kind of enjoyed being teased by her parents.

Just then the fireworks started around the opening ceremony venue called the Bird's Nest which kind of did look like a bird's nest. Mack watched in wonder at the two thousand and eight Chinese drummers, the movable printing blocks which turned out to have real people inside them, the karate masters, and the colorful dancers. A giant blue sphere appeared next. People, seeming to defy gravity, ran around it. Her jaw dropped open in wonder.

"How are they doing that?" She couldn't look away from the screen.

"I have no idea," her dad said, but just then the camera zoomed in and they saw that each runner was held by a cable. "Even with a cable, that's still got to be hard."

The parade of athletes began, and Mack read the names of countries she'd never heard of before. She felt like she didn't know much about the world at all. Some of the countries only had four or five athletes. She could only imagine the pressure on them to represent.

The United States finally entered the arena, and Mack leaned forward. "Look for the softball players, okay?"

"Okay," her mom said.

"Look, look, look." Mack pointed excitedly at the screen. "There's Jenny Finch. Wait, Mom, can you back that up? I think that was Cat Osterman right next to her."

Her mom pressed the rewind button and then made the image go forward in slow motion.

"Pause it. Pause it," Mack urged.

The pause was perfect, but since the camera was zoomed in so tightly on Jenny Finch there was no real way to tell who the other athlete was.

"I can't tell," Mack said disappointed. "That's okay. Maybe they'll show Cat later."

"They'll definitely show her when the games start." Her dad was obviously trying to make her feel better.

"That's true," Mack said. "I can wait, I guess." But still, she was a little disappointed.

After the ceremonies, Mack went to bed, but lay under the covers with her eyes wide open. There was no way she could sleep now. Were Cat Osterman and Jessica Mendoza having trouble sleeping, too? Beijing was so far away. Had they gotten used to the new time zone? Would the China team have the home field advantage like the Gators had against UCF? She frowned. That wasn't fair. But then again, Australia, Venezuela, Canada, and the Netherlands had a long way to travel, too. Well, maybe Australia didn't have that far to go, and Japan and Chinese Taipei weren't that far, either, but she hoped Team USA could deal with the traveling.

Her parents had told her that Chinese Taipei used to be called Taiwan, but the country decided to change its name. That was kind of cool, she thought. What if the United States decided to change its name all of a sudden to Washingtonland or Lincolnland? Maybe she'd ask the new history teacher she'd get in seventh grade why Chinese Taipei changed its name.

She wondered where she would travel to when she got selected for the 2016 Olympic softball team. The announcer said there were four cities still in the running to host the 2016 summer games—Madrid, Rio de Janeiro, Tokyo, and Chicago. She was nervous about going so far away from home, but decided not to think about the scary parts because by the time 2016 rolled around she'd be twenty years old and already in college.

She rolled over and pulled the covers up around her neck. She fell asleep imagining herself running onto the Olympic softball field with her fellow USA teammates, proud to represent her country in the gold medal game.

Chapter 32

Garbage Duty

Mack opened the car door before her mom turned off the engine.

"Hurry." She was glad her mom picked her up right after school. Sometimes she had to wait in the library until her mom or dad came at four-thirty, sometimes five.

"Okay, okay." Her mom rolled her eyes as she got out of the car. "We've got the game on the DVR. It's not going anywhere."

"I know, but if the softball team beats China then we'll be the only undefeated team, and we'll have the number one spot and a guaranteed medal. And besides, school's closed tomorrow because of Hurricane Fay and we might lose the electricity any second."

As soon as her mom unlocked the front door, Mack threw her backpack on the floor and grabbed the remote control. She turned on the TV and found the game in the list of recorded shows.

Her mom placed her briefcase on the floor next to Mack's discarded backpack. "You know, I think I'd like to watch the game with you."

"You would?"

"Sure. Can you just give me a minute to get dinner started? In fact, why don't you come in and peel the potatoes?"

Mack couldn't believe her mom was going to make her wait. She'd been waiting all day to see the game. It almost felt like her mom was stalling.

"We'll watch it as soon as you finish with those potatoes, okay?"

Mack sighed softly. "Okay."

She scrubbed the potatoes as fast as she could.

"So tell me more about your first day of seventh grade."

"It was okay."

"Just okay? Do you have any homework?"

"Just math, but it's easy."

"How was English?"

"Mrs. B is really nice." Mack started peeling the potatoes in the sink. "She grew up in India and has this really long last name, but she said we can call her Mrs. B."

Her mom laughed. "I saw Mrs. Balasubramanium's name on your schedule. I hope that won't be on a spelling test."

"I hope not, too." Mack laughed with her mom. "Mrs. B told me she talked with Mrs. Perez."

"Oh?"

"I guess she was trying to tell me she knows about my learning difference and knows I have extended time."

"And does Mrs. B know that my awesome child got a B in English last year?"

"I think so. I'm starting with Mrs. Perez tomorrow. Oh, no, I'm not. I guess I'll have to start on Thursday because of Hurricane Fay."

"You'll see Mrs. Perez two days a week this year, right?"

"Yeah." Mack finished peeling the last of the potatoes and rinsed them off. She held one up. "Do you want me to cut them?"

"Sure."

Mack cut the potatoes into cubes and put them in the pot her mom handed her. She put enough water in the pot to cover them. "Should I turn on the stove?"

"No, we'll wait for Daddy to get home."

Mack suddenly had a sinking feeling. Maybe her mom was going to make her wait until her dad got home to watch the game. That would be at five-thirty. Maybe they'd have to wait until after dinner. Her sinking feeling lasted all of two seconds because she heard her dad's key in the front door. The door squeaked open and he called, "Anybody home?"

Mack ran from the kitchen to the front door. She threw her arms around him in a quick hug. "What are you doing home?"

"The company told us to go home early and get ready for the hurricane." He put his briefcase and a black plastic bag on the floor. "But since we're stocked and ready, I think we should watch a softball game, don't you?"

"Yeah. Hey, Mom?" Mack called into the kitchen. "Can we watch the game now?"

Her mom came out of the kitchen. She kissed her husband and pointed at their lone offspring. "One track mind."

Her dad nodded as they stared at their daughter. "I remember something else she used to have a one-track mind about."

"What's that?" Mack's finger hovered over the play button on the remote control.

Her dad picked up the black bag. "This." He handed her the bag from Radio Shack.

Mack reluctantly put the remote control down and reached in. As soon as she wrapped her hand around the object she knew what it was.

"You guys. Really?"

Her parents nodded.

Mack pulled out her first ever cell phone. She threw the bag down, but held onto the phone tightly as she crushed her dad in a hug. "Thanks, Dad." She released her dad and gave her mom a tight hug, too. "Thanks, Mom."

"Your dad and I figured you were the only seventh grader without one so we decided to move up the schedule a bit and get you a phone now."

Mack turned the phone over and over in her hand, admiring the sleek design. "Thank you, thank you, thank you. I have to text Ashley right away." She turned the phone on and watched as the features powered up. "I have texting, don't I?"

Her dad smiled. "Yes, you have texting, but no Internet."

"That's okay. Thanks, Dad. Thanks, Mom." Mack typed a text to Ashley telling her she got a cell phone.

"Don't you want the instruction book?" her dad asked.

"C'mon. Only old people need those." She held the phone out. "Look, I already sent the text."

"She's a miracle kid," her mom said. "C'mon, we'll eat after the game."

Mack picked up the remote control and pushed the play button. She flopped down on the loveseat and reached for her jar of lucky sharks' teeth from the side table. So far Team USA was 6-0, and she wasn't going to chance fate by abandoning her jar of good luck anytime soon.

Her parents settled in to watch the game with her.

"Dad, do you think Cat'll pitch another no-hitter?"

"Maybe," her dad answered. "Or maybe she'll have a perfect game like Monica Abbott did against the Netherlands."

"Oh, that'd be awesome." Mack thought that would be the best thing ever.

"Didn't Team USA break the record for home runs or something?" her mom asked.

"Yeah, yeah, yeah," Mack answered excitedly. "Jessica Mendoza did it against the Netherlands. Her homer made twelve by one team in one Olympics which set the new record."

"Okay, so who do you think will hit the next home run?" her dad asked.

Mack thought about it for a second and decided to pick the player she hoped to play next to someday. "Jessica Mendoza."

"Do you want to bet garbage duty on that?" her dad asked with a gleam in his eye.

Mack loved a challenge. "Okay, but who are you picking?"

"You know I have to go with my girl, Crystl Bustos."

"Ah, I knew it. Okay, so if Mendoza hits the next home run then you have to take the garbage out for the next two weeks."

"Two whole weeks? Okay, but if Bustos jacks one then *you* have garbage duty."

"And if somebody else hits the next home run," her mom chimed in, "then you both have to cook dinner for me over the next two weeks. Starting tomorrow."

Mack and her dad looked at each other considering the bet.

"Okay," Mack said slowly, "but if Bustos or Mendoza hits the next home run you'll still cook for us, right?"

"It's a deal." Her mom grinned and settled back on the couch.

The USA softball team ran onto the field, and Mack's attention was riveted on Cat Osterman warming up in the circle.

The first batter up for China singled to center field and Mack groaned. "Well, there goes her no-hitter and her perfect game."

Two seconds later Mack got a text from Ashley, "r u watching?" Ashley must have turned the game on as soon as she got home, too.

Mack quickly texted back. "don't tell! we just started."

The top of the first inning ended without China scoring a run. "I can't believe China got two base runners. We might be in trouble this game."

Her dad nodded. "Let's hope Mendoza or Bustos settle our bet in the bottom of the first so we'll have at least one run. That'll calm their nerves and ours."

"Good plan, Dad."

Mack cheered loudly when Natasha Watley walked to lead off the inning for Team USA and then advanced to second base on a passed ball. She groaned when Caitlin Lowe struck out, but then her favorite left fielder got up to bat.

"Go Jessica. Home run. No garbage duty. No garbage duty," Mack chanted.

Mendoza got hit by a pitch, giving her a free pass to first base. Mack groaned because Bustos was up next. Mack practically held her breath when Bustos swung the bat sending the ball high in the air.

"Oh, no." Mack groaned and leaned forward.

The shortstop for the Chinese team settled under the pop and caught it.

Mack fell back against the cushions with an exaggerated sigh. "That was close."

"I almost had you," her dad said smugly.

Mack was both relieved, but torn. After weighing things in her mind for a few seconds, she ultimately decided that it was far more important for Team USA to score. Garbage duty wasn't so important all of a sudden.

"You know," her mom teased as Team USA's right fielder got up to bat, "Kelly Kretschman is a pretty awesome hitter, too. And

Stacey Nuveman has enough power to, what'd you call it, jack one out?"

Mack exchanged a glance with her dad. "I think we're in trouble."

Kelly Kretschman got up to bat with two runners on and one out. With one mighty swing of her bat, Kretschman slammed a three-run home run over the right field fence.

Mack jumped up. "We're winning three nothing. Happy Dance." She gyrated around the living room waving her arms. Then reality hit, and she froze. "Dad, we lost the bet."

Her dad sighed dramatically. "I know, I know. I wonder how your mom feels about peanut butter and jelly for two solid weeks."

Her mom laughed. "I'm sure you two can do better than that. And we're starting tomorrow."

Team USA had a good showing and put up a total of nine runs on the board. That was all they would need to win their last game of round-robin play. They shut out China by a score of 9-0.

Mack texted Ashley, "1-hitter!"

Ashley texted back, "team usa rules! vicky galindo got in the game!"

Mack texted, "happy dance for galindo! we play japan 2morrow."

"Wouldn't it be easier to just call Ashley?" Her mom called from the kitchen.

"Texting is way more fun," Mack yelled back.

"C'mon. Help me set the table."

"Okay," Mack said. She texted Ashley, "got 2 eat. c u later."

She powered down her phone and hugged it. Even though school had started again, things were really going her way. Well, except for the fact that she and her dad had to figure out how to cook, and fast.

Chapter 33

Silver Lining

Mack's dad paid the delivery girl and turned around holding several large plastic bags.

"Ladies," he said with a slight bow, "your dinner is served."

"Ah," her mom said as if impressed, "you two cooked Chinese tonight. How nice."

Mack relieved her dad of one of the bags. "Only the best for you, Mom. We figured you didn't want grits and eggs for dinner two nights in a row." She divvied up the cartons of food on the three TV trays. "Ashley said she'd start watching the game at her house at six o'clock, so hurry, Dad, it's almost six."

"She might text with some big news if we're not in sync?" Her dad rolled his eyes.

"Yeah, something like that." Mack sat down on the loveseat while her mom reached for the remote control. Even though the gold medal game had been played earlier in the day and the rest of the world already knew who had won, Mack didn't. She had been at school. Ashley, Halie, Marci, and the rest of the girls on the softball team, agreed not to discuss the game so they could go home and watch it without knowing the result. The only problem was having to wait for her dad to pick her up after school. She got her algebra homework done as she waited in the library, but that was about all she could do because she was way too excited to concentrate on anything else.

In her very first session of the year with Mrs. Perez that morning, Mack admitted she was nervous about the workload in seventh grade.

Mrs. Perez told her, "The journey of a thousand miles starts with a single step." She said that, yes, it would be quite a journey dealing with dyslexia in seventh grade, but a positive attitude about the journey was the all-important first step toward success.

Mack finished a forkful of General Tso's Chicken. "I can't believe we have to play Japan again. Maybe Yukiko Ueno is still tired after pitching all those extra-inning games against us and Australia."

Her dad agreed. "Ueno is one of the best pitchers in the world, but my girl Bustos came through with a three-run homer in the ninth to win that semi-final game. I wish we'd bet for garbage duty on that game."

Her mom held up her tray of Chinese food. "I'm glad you two bet on the China game instead."

Mack smiled at her mom and then turned back to watch Cat Osterman warm up in the pitcher's circle. She was proud that number eight was starting the gold medal game for Team USA.

Cat threw the first pitch. Ball one. Mack's heart sank for a moment, but then three pitches later, Osterman struck out the first Japanese batter of the inning.

Mack pumped a fist in the air. "Yes." Just then her cell phone chimed. It was a text from Ashley.

"dude, did u start?"

Mack texted back, "yes. 1 down."

After waiting three long seconds, Ashley texted, "same."

Her mom chuckled. "You two are so fast at that. Texting should be an Olympic sport."

"Ashley would win the gold, for sure. I'd only get the silver."

"Silver's still okay, though," her dad said.

"Pfft, not really. It's the first loser."

"I have to disagree with you, Stinky. Silver means you're the second best in the entire world. That's not too shabby."

"I guess." But Mack didn't really believe it.

Her dad shook his head. "So I guess it's gold or nothing when you play in the 2016 Olympics."

"Ooh," Mack groaned as the Japan batter swung big but missed for the second out of the inning. "Of course. What else?"

Her mom frowned. "Two more years of middle school, four years of high school, and what, two years of college before then?"

"Yeah, eight long years before I go to Madrid or Rio de Janeiro or Tokyo or all the way to Chicago."

"Eight years," her mom repeated. "Maybe we shouldn't put so much pressure on ourselves this early." She glared at Mack's dad.

"But, Mom," Mack said, "the journey of a thousand miles starts with a single step."

Both of her parents chuckled.

"Mrs. Perez?" her mom asked.

Mack nodded. "But with that stupid IOC Committee voting softball out, it feels like we've got the bases loaded with no way to score."

Her mom nodded in sympathy. "Like you're all dressed up with no where to go."

"Yeah." Mack suddenly lost her appetite.

"Hey," her dad said, "don't get depressed. A lot can happen between now and then, so stay positive and—what did Mrs. Perez say—make lemonade. Maybe the rest of the world will catch up to Team USA by 2016."

"Maybe." Mack picked up her food again. "I hope so. Japan is really good. So is Australia."

"See?" her dad said. "And, uh, we haven't won the gold medal yet. Maybe we shouldn't take this Japan team too lightly."

Mack hadn't even considered anything besides a gold medal for Team USA. Her stomach did a quick flip. What if Team USA lost? There was no double elimination like in the College World Series, so if they lost they would only get the silver medal. She took a deep breath and willed Natasha Watley to get on base.

The Japanese pitcher, Ueno, couldn't get a handle on Watley's slap hit and Watley reached first base safely. Mack cheered and then let herself relax. But just a little.

"Bunt, Caitlin, bunt," Mack called to Team USA's center fielder stepping into the batter's box.

Lowe slapped a slow roller to the second baseman, but Lowe was too fast and reached first base safely.

Mack did a tiny happy dance on the couch. There were two runners on with no outs.

"C'mon, Jessica," Mack called to her favorite left fielder and shook her jar of lucky sharks' teeth. Much to her disappointment Mendoza hit into a fielder's choice forcing Natasha Watley out at third.

"Dad, here's your girl." Mack pointed at Crystl Bustos stepping into the batter's box.

His mouth was full of egg roll, so he just nodded and threw her a thumbs-up.

Bustos hit a slow bouncer to the second baseman who backhanded the ball softly to the shortstop. Her toss was a little too soft, though, and the speedy Mendoza was safe at second, allowing Team USA to load the bases with only one out.

"bases loaded," came a text from Ashley.

"usa rools," Mack texted back, but was pretty sure she had spelled the word wrong. She shrugged. Texting wasn't an exact science, and Ashley wouldn't care, but she made a mental note to check the spelling after the game.

"Ah, my favorite player," her mom said as Kelly Kretschman came up to bat. Kretschman quickly hit into a fielder's choice, forcing Lowe out at home. "Oh, well. She's still my favorite."

Andrea Duran, Team USA's third baseman, popped up to the catcher to end the inning.

Mack groaned. "Do you see how frustrating that is? We had bases loaded and couldn't score."

"Chin up, Mack," her dad said, "we've got six more innings."

In the top of the third inning, Japan scored the first run of the game with a lead-off double, sacrifice bunt, and a single up the middle. Mack got a sick feeling in her stomach when the top of the order for Team USA went down without scoring in the bottom of the third.

In the top of the fourth inning, Mack's stomach problems intensified as the lead-off batter for Japan belted a home run over the center field fence putting them up by a score of 2-0. Mack got a little relief when Crystl Bustos led off the bottom of the fourth with her own solo home run over the right field fence to move Team USA within one run.

The score remained 2-1 in Japan's favor as Caitlin Lowe led off the bottom of the sixth inning for Team USA.

"Just get on base," Mack willed. Lowe slammed a base hit into right field.

"What do you think?" her dad asked as Jessica Mendoza got up to bat. "Swing away or bunt?"

Mack shrugged. "Well, Mendoza can smack it, but we really need to score a run to tie. I say bunt . . . I think."

Mendoza squared to bunt and sacrificed herself on the third pitch to move Lowe to second base.

"Good call," her dad said. "Now we just have to get her home. Guess who's up again."

Mack crossed her fingers and prayed and prayed that Bustos would hit another home run. If Team USA could go into the seventh inning ahead by one run, they would only need three outs to win the gold medal.

"What are they doing, Dad?"

"Looks like they're intentionally walking Bustos. I don't blame them."

Mack sank into the cushions on the loveseat. How could they just walk Bustos like that? Chickens. Bustos was supposed to hit another home run. Bustos jogged to first base on ball four. Mack's mom's favorite player stepped into the batter's box and promptly walked to load the bases. Mack cheered up. A little. With Kretschman on first base, Bustos on second, and Lowe on third, Andrea Duran stepped into the batter's box with only one out.

"C'mon, Andrea," Mack cheered through gritted teeth. "Just a little single. Or a sac fly. I don't care. Just get Caitlin in to score."

Duran popped out to the shortstop, and Mack groaned.

Stacey Nuveman, Team USA's catcher, got up to bat. Nuveman had enough power to hit one out. Mack crossed her fingers. Nuveman swung the bat and made contact. Mack leaned forward. The second baseman caught the pop up for the third out. Mack slid all the way off the couch onto the rug.

"Again. Bases loaded and we couldn't score. Ahh! This is so not fair."

"I'm with you," her mom said. "This is nerve-wracking."

Mack resettled on the loveseat only to watch Japan add insult to injury by scoring a third run with a hit and run play in the top of the seventh inning giving them a 3-1 lead. Texts to and from Ashley became more frantic as they digitally worried about the outcome.

Mack sat forward when Vicky Galindo led off the top of the seventh with a pinch-hit single. It was now or never. Team USA had to score two runs to tie, three to win.

Three quick outs later, Team USA went down in defeat.

Mack sat back stunned. She set her not-so-lucky sharks' teeth on the side table. Team USA had just lost the gold medal game.

A text came in from Ashley, but Mack couldn't bring herself to read it. She was still trying to figure out what had just happened. This wasn't the way it was supposed to be.

"I know you're disappointed," her mom said. "I am, too, but think of all those young girls in Japan whose Olympic heroes just won a gold medal for the first time in their country. Maybe . . . maybe it's okay to let someone else have it this time."

"Hey, Stinky, maybe there's a silver lining—"

"Dad, don't say silver."

Her dad chuckled. "Okay, but they keep saying that Team USA dominates. Maybe they can't say that anymore." He gestured toward the screen. "Maybe eight years from now, you'll be on that team restoring gold to the United States."

Mack made a silent wish. She wished that Team USA would stay strong and play well in all the other big tournaments around the world—the World Cups, the Pan Am Games, and those International Softball Federation tournaments. She hoped Team USA could keep those bases loaded until she was old enough and good enough to play on the team.

Epilogue

Mackenzie Kelly took a deep breath and stretched her five-foot-nine inch frame before sitting down at her computer. She wanted to blog one last time before heading out.

She opened up her blog site and with her hands poised above the keyboard, stopped to think. With so many things racing through her mind, it was difficult to force herself to slow down. She laughed. Way back in middle school, Mrs. Perez always told her to take a second to regroup before diving into things. She suddenly knew where she had to start. She lowered her hands on the keyboard.

> Many of you may not know this, but I got kicked off the softball team in sixth grade. Can you believe it? Yeah, I was pretty much failing English, but that was the year I learned I had dyslexia. It was the year I learned that having dyslexia meant I had to work extra hard just to keep up with my classmates. To be honest, it's still something I have to work on to this day (thank goodness for spell check!), but back then I threw everything into learning strategies to help me overcome my "different wiring." Although it seemed like it took a million years, I finally got reinstated on the team and haven't missed a day since. (Okay there was that one ankle injury in tenth grade, but other than that . . .)
>
> I had a lot of other things on my mind back then in sixth grade, too. Not only did I get kicked off the team, but UCF (that's where I went to college as most of you know) got beaten by the University of Florida Gators in their first trip to the College World Series, Team USA got beaten by Japan for the gold medal in the 2008 Beijing Olympic Games, and (as far as I knew back then) there

would be no more softball in the Olympics after the 2008 Games. All of that was a lot to put on a kid of twelve, but I realized something that year. I learned that with patience and hard work I could pretty much tackle anything.

Mack's hands rested on the keyboard. She missed the good old days of middle school. Things were happening so fast lately that she didn't have much time to visit with any of her old friends. She hadn't seen much of Taylor, Halie, Marci, or even Ashley during the past few years.

Ashley lived out her dream playing second base at Florida State and took a position in the business office of her dad's construction firm. Halie pitched at Georgia Tech, quite happily, and became a fourth grade teacher somewhere in Atlanta. Marci gave up softball after high school, but went to UCF with Mack. In fact, Marci was still at UCF pursuing a Master's degree in Environmental Engineering. Mack got a handful of emails from Taylor over the years, but had pretty much lost track of her when Taylor's family moved to New York following her graduation from Winterford High School. Taylor played softball at a university called Stony Brook, but Mack had never heard of it.

Mack sighed at the memories. She put her hands back on the keyboard and continued.

> I've made a lot of friends through softball. Friends through my middle and high school teams, friends through UCF, and a ton of friends through my association with Team USA.
>
> As I write this blog I realize how absolutely blessed I am to be part of Team USA softball that is finally getting the chance to bring Olympic Gold back home. My heart broke when softball was not reinstated to the Olympic Games for 2016, but I know how fortunate I am to have been a part of the twelve year movement that finally got softball back for 2020.

And you, all of you, are the reason I have an Olympics to go to. People like Jamie Gray, who at age thirteen or fourteen started that savesoftball.com website. Other websites, like backsoftball.com helped raise awareness worldwide, too. So many of you have helped, and all I can say is thank you. I wouldn't be here without you.

Oh, I just thought of something. A lot of you have emailed me wanting to know why I wear number forty-four on Team USA, but not for UCF. I wore number eight at UCF in honor of Cat Osterman (she's Team USA's pitching coach now—but you all knew that, didn't you?). Cat wouldn't like it if I stole her old number on Team USA, so I proudly wear number forty-four in honor of Laura Berg (AKA Grandma) who roamed the outfield for Team USA in four consecutive Olympic games. I wanted to break her record and play in at least five, but since softball wasn't voted in for the 2016 Olympics, I'm a little behind schedule. But, hey, like I said—if you're patient and work hard, good things will happen.

Oh, on a side note, Cat was disappointed when I told her that way back in sixth grade, I wanted to go to the University of Texas, but then I caught Golden Knight fever that same year and ended up at UCF. Sorry Cat. She's still faster than me at texting, though!

As soon as I finish this blog, I'm heading out to meet the team because we leave for the 2020 Olympic Games tonight. My suitcases and equipment bags are packed and sitting by the front door. My mom keeps crying, but I think it's a good kind of crying. She and Dad have always been my number one fans!

I don't know if I'll have time to blog while I'm there, but I know you'll all be with me in spirit.

And remember: When life throws you a curve ball— SWING!

Mack posted her blog, powered down her laptop, and headed to the front door to start the adventure she'd been dreaming about since sixth grade.

ABOUT THE AUTHOR

Barbara L. Clanton is a native New Yorker who left those "New York minutes" for the slower-paced palm-tree-filled life in Orlando, Florida. While still in school she played any sport she could find: softball, volleyball, basketball, and field hockey. During high school, she could even be found in the upstairs gym playing team handball with her friends. She played softball at Princeton and was the captain her senior year. She is a retired mathematics teacher and has coached both softball and basketball in both New York and Florida. She still plays softball, but has picked up a new hobby! "Dr. Barb" plays bass guitar in a pop-rock band called The Flounders. Her writing credits so far include four young adult novels from Regal Crest Enterprises, LLC. *Out of Left Field: Marlee's Story, Art for Art's Sake: Meredith's Story, Quite an Undertaking: Devon's Story*, and *Tools of Ignorance: Lisa's Story. Bases Loaded* is her other Title IX novel from Dragonfeather Books. Visit her website at www.BLClanton.com.

www.ingramcontent.com/pod-product-compliance
Lightning Source LLC
Chambersburg PA
CBHW031941070426
42450CB00005BA/305